Neurofunctional Prudence and Morality

Philosophers across many traditions have long theorized about the relationship between prudence and morality. Few clear answers have emerged, however, in large part because of the inherently speculative nature of traditional philosophical methods. This book aims to forge a bold new path forward, outlining a theory of prudence and morality that unifies a wide variety of findings in neuroscience with philosophically sophisticated normative theorizing.

The author summarizes the emerging behavioral neuroscience of prudence and morality, showing how human moral and prudential cognition and motivation are known to involve over a dozen brain regions and capacities. He then outlines a detailed philosophical theory of prudence and morality based on neuroscience and lived human experience. The result demonstrates how this theory coheres with and explains the behavioral neuroscience, showing how each brain region and capacity interact to give rise to prudential and moral behavior.

Neurofunctional Prudence and Morality: A Philosophical Theory will be of interest to philosophers and psychologists working in moral psychology, neuroethics, and decision theory.

Marcus Arvan is Associate Professor of Philosophy at the University of Tampa. He has published widely on ethical theory, nonideal justice, human rights, and metaphysics. He published his first book, *Rightness as Fairness: A Moral and Political Theory*, in 2016.

Routledge Focus on Philosophy

Routledge Focus on Philosophy is an exciting and innovative new series, capturing and disseminating some of the best and most exciting new research in philosophy in short book form. Peer reviewed and at a maximum of fifty thousand words shorter than the typical research monograph, *Routledge Focus on Philosophy* titles are available in both ebook and print on demand format. Tackling big topics in a digestible format the series opens up important philosophical research for a wider audience, and as such is invaluable reading for the scholar, researcher, and student seeking to keep their finger on the pulse of the discipline. The series also reflects the growing interdisciplinarity within philosophy and will be of interest to those in related disciplines across the humanities and social sciences.

Totalitarianism and Philosophy
Alan Haworth

The Repugnant Conclusion
A Philosophical Inquiry
Christopher Cowie

Confucianism and the Philosophy of Well-Being
Richard Kim

Neurofunctional Prudence and Morality
A Philosophical Theory
Marcus Arvan

For more information about this series, please visit: www.routledge.com/Routledge-Focus-on-Philosophy/book-series/RFP

Neurofunctional Prudence and Morality
A Philosophical Theory

Marcus Arvan

NEW YORK AND LONDON

First published 2020 by Routledge

2 Park Square, Milton Park, Abingdon, Oxon OX14 4RN
605 Third Avenue, New York, NY 10017

Routledge is an imprint of the Taylor & Francis Group, an informa business

First issued in paperback 2022

Copyright © 2020 Taylor & Francis

The right of Marcus Arvan to be identified as author of this work has been asserted by him in accordance with sections 77 and 78 of the Copyright, Designs and Patents Act 1988.

Chapter 3 of this book is available for free in PDF format as Open Access from the individual product page at www.routledge.com. It has been made available under a Creative Commons Attribution-Non Commercial-No Derivatives 4.0 license.

All rights reserved. No part of this book may be reprinted or reproduced or utilised in any form or by any electronic, mechanical, or other means, now known or hereafter invented, including photocopying and recording, or in any information storage or retrieval system, without permission in writing from the publishers.

Notice:
Product or corporate names may be trademarks or registered trademarks, and are used only for identification and explanation without intent to infringe.

Publisher's Note

The publisher has gone to great lengths to ensure the quality of this reprint but points out that some imperfections in the original copies may be apparent.

Library of Congress Cataloging-in-Publication Data
A catalog record for this title has been requested

ISBN: 978-0-367-23015-9 (hbk)
ISBN: 978-1-03-233703-6 (pbk)
DOI: 10.4324/9780429277955

Typeset in Times New Roman
by codeMantra

Contents

List of Figures		vi
Acknowledgments		vii
	Introduction	1
1	Outline of the Emerging Behavioral Neuroscience of Prudence and Morality	8
2	Outline of a Theory of Prudence	26
3	Derivation of Morality from Prudence	60
4	A Unified Neurofunctional Theory of Prudence and Morality?	95
5	Replies to Potential Concerns, and Avenues for Future Research	125
	Index	139

Figures

2.1	Childhood Moral-Prudential Learning	39
2.2	Adolescent Moral-Prudential Consolidation	41
2.3	Adult Categorical Moral-Prudential Consolidation	44
2.4	Outline of a Normative Theory of Prudence	46
2.5	A Descriptive Model of Prudential Psychology	50
3.1	Outline of a Unified Normative Theory of Prudence, Morality, and Justice	86
3.2	A Unified Descriptive Model of Prudential and Moral Psychology	88

Acknowledgments

I thank M.L. Arvan, Dan Dennett, Trevor Hedberg, Timothy Jussaume, Laura Kane, David Killoren, Justin Klocksiem, Josh May, Christopher Noble, Greg Robson, Matt Stichter, Eleonora Viganò, Andrés Carlos Luco, and three other referees for their helpful feedback, as well as Andrew Weckenmann, the editorial board, and staff at Routledge. My deepest thanks are to Maryana and my family for their love and support.

Introduction

Prudence involves making rational decisions regarding one's own life and well-being.[1] In contrast, morality is normally thought to be a social code of conduct concerned with how our actions affect both ourselves and others—defining what is good, evil, right, and wrong.[2] These apparent differences give rise to the age-old question of how prudence and morality relate. Many have argued that moral behavior is always or usually prudent. For example, in Plato's works, Socrates repeatedly argues that the 'just' person has a well-ordered, happy soul.[3] Similarly, Aristotle argued that moral virtues are necessary for *eudaimonia*, or personal flourishing over a complete life.[4] Analogous ideas exist in Epicureanism,[5] Stoicism,[6] and Confucianism,[7] and in religious traditions ranging from Buddhism[8] to Judaism,[9] Christianity,[10] and Islam.[11] Then, there is the contractarian tradition, which holds that prudence requires upholding a social contract comprising moral principles.[12] However, many remain skeptical of whether moral behavior is usually or always prudent.[13] Finally, others argue that even if moral behavior is always or usually prudent, prudence and morality involve fundamentally different kinds of normative reasons.[14]

Until now, philosophers have primarily approached these questions using traditional philosophical methods—that is, various forms of armchair argumentation.[15] However, as the above disagreements illustrate, philosophers often disagree deeply from the armchair. This raises the question of whether there is a better philosophical method for investigating prudence and morality. This book argues that there is—that if we use rigorous principles of theory selection adapted from scientific fields of inquiry and combine armchair reflection with behavioral neuroscience, we can see that our philosophical and empirical evidence together *converge* upon a new, unified normative and descriptive theory of prudence and morality.

2 Introduction

The theory this book defends through this new method is both descriptive and normative. First, it is a *normative philosophical theory* of how people ought to act to behave prudently and morally. Second, it is a *descriptive neurofunctional theory* of how prudent and moral agents actually think and act. This book argues that the theory outlined is not only normatively attractive from the armchair but also the best current explanation of known behavioral neuroscience.

Chapter 1 provides a brief overview of the emerging behavioral neuroscience of prudence and morality, showing how prudential and moral cognition are known to involve 17 brain regions and associated capacities and dispositions ranging from episodic memory to mental time-travel, other-perspective-taking, counterfactual-prediction, emotion-processing, fear-conditioning, and risk-aversion.

Chapter 2 then outlines and refines a normative theory of prudence previously sketched in my 2016 book *Rightness as Fairness: A Moral and Political Theory*.[16] I argue, first, that prudence is a matter of acting in ways that make one's life go well as a whole. I then use a variety of examples from history, art, and different cultures— along with a developmental model of moral and prudential learning across childhood and adulthood—to argue that normatively prudent individuals typically internalize a very specific form of '*moral risk-aversion*'[17] as a high-level constraint on first-order prudential deliberation.[18]

Chapter 3 then argues that this theory of prudence entails a novel theory of morality: namely, a revised version of theory I previously defended in *Rightness as Fairness: A Moral and Political Theory*. I detail, first, how Chapter 2's theory entails that it is prudent to obey a fundamental moral principle: the Categorical-Instrumental Imperative.[19] I then detail how this principle entails a moral decision-procedure: a Moral Original Position similar to, but more general than, John Rawls's famous model of justice.[20] Next, I demonstrate how Four Principles of Fairness can be derived from this model and be combined into a criterion of moral rightness: Rightness as Fairness.[21] Finally, Chapter 3 uses this book's theory of prudence to provide a new defense of these derivations, defending Rightness as Fairness against previous critiques and revising Rightness as Fairness's implications for social and political philosophy. Here, I argue that prudence—and by extension morality— requires adopting a series of Social-Political Original Positions to correctly apply Rightness as Fairness to institutions, individuals, and groups in ideal and nonideal social-political conditions.[22]

Chapter 4 then argues that this book's unified theory of prudence and morality explains the behavioral neuroscience summarized in Chapter 1 better than existing alternatives—both as a normative explanation of *why* various capacities should be involved in moral and prudential cognition, and as a descriptive neurofunctional explanation of *how* prudential and moral cognition actually work.

Finally, Chapter 5 addresses potential concerns, including potential counterexamples to my theory of prudence, as well as concerns that the theory is overly speculative, commits the naturalistic fallacy, violates the 'is-ought gap', and at most gives prudential reasons for moral behavior.

Before proceeding, I want to make several important notes about this book's method, scope, and understanding of the relationship between normative philosophy and the empirical sciences.

First, a note about method. It is standard in academic philosophy to seek 'rigorous' arguments, where this is broadly understood as taking utmost care to ensure that every argumentative premise is true or highly plausible, and each inference deductively valid or inductively cogent. Although this book defends the plausibility of its theory, it takes a different approach. My method is to lay out the theory in its entirety, and then argue that the theory satisfies *Seven Principles of Theory Selection*[23] better than alternatives. Although this method departs from standard philosophical practice, I have argued that it is epistemically more rigorous than standard philosophical methods.[24] For, as noted earlier, standard philosophical methods have clear limitations. Because different philosophers often disagree over which premises are true or plausible, as well as over which inferences are valid or cogent, 'rigorous' philosophical argumentation as standardly understood tends to generate a multiplicity of incompatible arguments and theories.[25] I have argued that to resolve this problem—to determine which theories are actually true—philosophy should instead utilize principles of theory selection adapted from the sciences. Hence, this will be my method here. Although I believe each chapter's arguments are plausible, my method will not be to rigorously establish each premise or inference. Instead, I will move quickly, laying out the book's theory and then returning in Chapter 4 to the question of how well it satisfies principles of theory selection. Readers are then invited to judge whether this is the best method.

Second, a note on this book's scope. This book does not purport to provide a complete and exhaustive examination of the behavioral neuroscience of prudential and moral psychology—a monumental task that might overwhelm readers. Although I hope to pursue this larger task in future work, this book's aim is to *outline* how its theory explains a variety of philosophical and empirical phenomena better than alternative normative moral theories and theories of moral psychology. If this book is successful, it will have made a compelling case that its theory warrants further attention and investigation by philosophers and empirical scientists.

Finally, a note on how this book understands normativity in relation to empirical science. As Chapter 5 explains, some theorists deny that there can be fruitful cooperation between the empirical sciences and normative philosophy—the argument being that empirical and normative phenomena are fundamentally different in kind. This book argues that even if the empirical and normative are different in kind, there are nevertheless normative epistemic reasons to believe that empirical science *is* relevant to evaluating normative theories of prudence and morality.

This book theorizes about four types of normativity: prudential, moral, teleofunctional, and epistemic. Chapter 2 argues that prudential normativity requires acting in ways that have the best-expected outcomes for the agent acting. Chapter 3 then argues that moral normativity—understood as a general normative requirement to justify our actions to others—can be derived from prudential normativity. Chapter 4 then argues that normative theories of prudence and morality have two types of implications relevant to empirical science:

1 Normative teleofunctional implications regarding which brain regions, capacities, and dispositions *should* play particular functional purposes (or 'telos') in prudential and moral cognition; and by extension,
2 Empirical psychological predictions about what science *will in fact* observe when people think and behave as they normatively should.

In other words, Chapter 4 argues that normative theories entail both normative *and* empirical predictions. Finally, Chapter 4 argues that epistemic normativity, embodied in seven principles of theory selection, reveals that we should evaluate normative theories in light of all of their implications—both normative and empirical—arguing in turn that this book's theory explains Chapter 1's behavioral neuroscience better than alternatives.

This book's theory may or may not be wholly accurate. Given the limited but rapidly growing state of behavioral neuroscience, it would be surprising if the theory turns out to be descriptively correct in every detail. Similarly, given how much normative disagreement exists in moral philosophy, the theory is sure to be normatively controversial. However, few theories—either in the sciences or in philosophy—are accurate in every detail. The real test at any given time is comparative, that is, whether a given theory predicts and explains target phenomena better than alternatives. This book argues that its theory is currently the most compelling explanation of a variety of descriptive and normative phenomena. If this is correct, then the theory warrants further research and attention.

Notes

1 Bricker (1980), Bykvist (2013).
2 Gert and Gert (2017), Scanlon (1998).
3 Plato [2010]: *The Republic*, Books IV, IX; *Gorgias* 496–9.
4 Aristotle [1984]: *Nicomachean Ethics*, Book II, §§6–9, Book IV §§5, 11–13, Book X.
5 Epicurus [2014]: *Letter to Menoceus*, §E.
6 Epictetus [1865]: *Enchiridion*, Chapter 1, §2; Aurelius [1862]: *Meditations*: Book IV, §8.
7 Yu (2007).
8 Goodman (2017): §1.
9 *The Talmud* [2019]: Tractate Shabbos 30b.
10 *The New American Bible* [2011]: Psalms 1, Proverbs 2–3, 10–22, Wisdom of Ben Sira, Mark 5: 3–10. Cf. Mattison (2008).
11 *The Qur'an* [2015]: 16:97.
12 Gauthier (1986), Hobbes [1651], Kavka [1985].
13 Joyce (2007): §3.2, Nietzsche [1887], Sumner (1998).
14 Kant [1785], Luco (2016), Prichard (1912).
15 Barcalow (2007): 14–5, Timmons (2007): 27–31, Vaughn (2009): 46–7.
16 Arvan (2016): Chapters 2 and 3, 65–7, 93–115.
17 As Chapter 2 explains, the form of 'moral risk-aversion' I defend is not strictly-speaking risk-averse, at least as technically understood in decision-theory, viz. preferring a less-desirable but more certain outcome over a more desirable yet more uncertain one (Peterson 2017: Chapter 10). My account holds that normatively prudent agents engage in behavior that *looks* like risk-aversion—specifically, aversion to risking the potential costs of violating moral norms—because prudent agents learn to treat the expected long-term benefits of moral actions to be greater. Although technically this is self-control (choosing greater long-term benefits over lesser short-term ones), I call it 'moral risk-aversion' to highlight the intuitive sense in which agents with the attitudes I describe avoid 'risking' immoral behavior.
18 Cf. Arvan (2016): Chapter 2. Readers may wonder how my theory relates to Viganò's (2015, 2017a, 2017b) project of providing neuroscientific evidence for an updated version of Adam Smith's [1759] theory of prudence. Whereas Viganò holds that general forms of risk-aversion

are prudent (Viganò 2017a: 223–4), I argue that normatively prudent behavior involves a much more specific set of negative categorical attitudes that aim to avoid any possibility of regret in morally salient cases, as well as positive categorical attitudes that acting on these negative attitudes has the best-expected lifetime outcomes.
19 Arvan (2016): Chapters 3 and 4.
20 Ibid.: Chapter 5. Cf. Rawls (1999).
21 Arvan (2016): Chapter 6.
22 Ibid.: Chapter 7.
23 Ibid.: 3.
24 Ibid.: Chapter 1, §§1–2.
25 Ibid.: Brennan (2010).

References

Aristotle [1984]. *The Complete Works of Aristotle: The Revised Oxford Translation*. J. Barnes (Ed.). Princeton: Princeton University Press.
Arvan, M. (2016). *Rightness as Fairness: A Moral and Political Theory*. New York: Palgrave Macmillan.
Aurelius, M. [1862]. *Meditations*. G. Long (trans.). Logos Publishing, 2018.
Barcalow, E. (2007). *Moral Philosophy: Theories and Issues*, 4th edition. Belmont: Thomson Wadsworth.
Brennan, J. (2010). Scepticism about Philosophy. *Ratio*, *23*(1), 1–16.
Bricker, P. (1980). Prudence. *Journal of Philosophy*, *77*(7), 381–401.
Bykvist, K. (2013). Prudence. *International Encyclopedia of Ethics*. H. Lafollette (Ed.). doi:10.1002/9781444367072.wbiee590.
Epictetus [1865]. *The Complete Works of Epictetus*. E. Carter (Ed.). Cambridge: Little, Brown, and Company.
Epicurus [2014]. *The Essential Epicurus: Letters, Principal Doctrines, Vatican Sayings, and Fragments*. E. O'Connor (Trans.), London: The Big Nest.
Gauthier, D. (1987). *Morals by Agreement*. Oxford: Oxford University Press.
Gert, B. & Gert, J. (2017). The Definition of Morality. In E.N. Zalta (ed.), *The Stanford Encyclopedia of Philosophy*. https://plato.stanford.edu/archives/fall2017/entries/morality-definition/.
Goodman, C. (2017). Ethics in Indian and Tibetan Buddhism. In E.N. Zalta (ed.), *The Stanford Encyclopedia of Philosophy*. https://plato.stanford.edu/archives/spr2017/entries/ethics-indian-buddhism/.
Hobbes, T. [1651]. *Leviathan*. In Sir W. Molesworth (ed.), *The English Works of Thomas Hobbes: Now First Collected and Edited*, Volume 3, London: John Bohn, 1839–45, ix–714.
Joyce, R. (2007). *The Myth of Morality*. Cambridge: Cambridge University Press.
Kant, I. [1785]. *Groundwork of the Metaphysics of Morals*. In M.J. Gregor (ed.), *The Cambridge Edition of the Works of Immanuel Kant: Practical Philosophy*. Cambridge: Cambridge University Press, 1996, 38–108.

Kavka, G.S. [1984]. The Reconciliation Project. In R. Shafer-Landau (ed.), *Ethical Theory: An Anthology*. Malden: Blackwell, 2007, 160–73.
Luco, A.C. (2016). Non-Negotiable: Why Moral Naturalism Cannot Do Away With Categorical Reasons. *Philosophical Studies, 173*(9), 2511–28.
Mattison III, W.C. (2008). *Introducing Moral Theology: True Happiness and the Virtues*. Grand Rapids: Brazos Press.
Nietzsche, F.W. [1887]. *On the Genealogy of Morals*. Oxford: Oxford Paperbacks, 2009.
Plato [2010]. *Dialogues of Plato: Translated Into English, with Analyses and Introduction*. B. Jowett (Trans.). New York: Cambridge University Press, 2010.
Prichard, H.A. (1912). Does Moral Philosophy Rest on a Mistake? *Mind, 21*(81): 21–37.
Rawls, J. (1999). *A Theory of Justice: Revised Edition*. Cambridge, MA: The Belknap Press of Harvard University Press.
Scanlon, T.M. (1998). *What We Owe to Each Other*. Cambridge, MA: Harvard University Press.
Smith, A. [1759]. *The Theory of Moral Sentiments*, D.D. Raphael and A.L. Macfie (eds.), *Vol. I of the Glasgow Edition of the Works and Correspondence of Adam Smith*, Indianapolis: Liberty Fund, 1982.
Sumner, L.W. (1998). Is Virtue Its Own Reward? *Social Philosophy and Policy, 15*(1), 18–36.
The New American Bible [2011]. Revised Edition. New Jersey: World Catholic Press.
The Qur'an [2015]. M.A.S. Abdel Haleem (Trans.). Oxford: Oxford University Press.
The Talmud [2019]. Tractate Shabbat. Jewish Virtual Library: https://www.jewishvirtuallibrary.org/tractate-shabbat, retrieved 3 June 2019.
Timmons, M. (2007). *Disputed Moral Issues: A Reader*. New York: Oxford University Press.
Vaughn, L. (2009). *Bioethics: Principles, Issues, and Cases*. Oxford: Oxford University Press.
Viganò, E. (2017a). Adam Smith's Theory of Prudence Updated with Neuroscientific and Behavioral Evidence. *Neuroethics, 10*(2), 215–33.
―――― (2017b). Not Just an Inferior Virtue, nor Self-Interest: Adam Smith on Prudence. *Journal of Scottish Philosophy, 15*(1), 125–43.
―――― (2015). *Smithian Prudence and Its Relevance in Moral Philosophy and Neuroscience*, PhD dissertation, Università Vita-Salute San Raffaele, https://www.academia.edu/28573514/Smithian_Prudence_and_its_Relevance_in_Moral_Philosophy_and_Neuroscience, retrieved 20 June 2018.
Yu, J. (2007). *The Ethics of Confucius and Aristotle: Mirrors of Virtue*. New York: Routledge.

1 Outline of the Emerging Behavioral Neuroscience of Prudence and Morality

This chapter provides a brief overview of the emerging behavioral neuroscience of prudence and morality. My purposes here are twofold. First, the findings present normative questions: why *should* various brain regions and capacities found to be involved in moral and prudential cognition be involved? Why not other brain regions or capacities? Second, the findings raise empirical questions, namely, *how* do various brain regions and capacities function and interact to generate normatively prudent and moral behavior? Chapters 2 and 3 will provide a unified normative and descriptive theory of prudence and morality. Chapter 4 then argues that the theory is currently the most compelling normative and descriptive explanation of the behavioral neuroscience now summarized.

Before beginning, several points warrant clarification. First, this chapter does not presuppose neuroessentialism, the view that specific capacities are essential to or located in particular brain regions. This chapter merely reports which capacities have been found to be empirically *associated* with various brain regions. Second, although I aim to err on the side of completeness, I will not summarize every capacity associated with every brain region discussed. Because brain regions are typically associated with many functions, some having no clear bearing on prudential or moral cognition, discussing every known function would be unwieldy and distracting. Consequently, although I aim to provide a complete summary, I will in some cases focus selectively on capacities that have a *prima facie* claim to relevance to morality and prudence, noting additional known brain-region functions in the chapter's notes.

1 Mental Time-Travel

Mental time-travel, the capacity to *imaginatively simulate* different possible pasts and futures,[1] appears to be central to moral responsibility and performance.[2] First, human adults—who we ordinarily consider to be fully responsible moral agents—typically have robust mental time-travel capacities.[3] Second, subclasses of human beings who exhibit diminished moral capacities—children, adolescents, and psychopaths[4]—have substantially underdeveloped mental time-travel neural-circuitry,[5] making them less able to appreciate the consequences of their actions.[6] Third, mental time-travel is linked to moral performance: (1) lack of imaginative vividness of the future predicts criminal delinquency[7] and psychopathy,[8] (2) the ability to project oneself into the future is negatively related to unethical behavior,[9] (3) experimental interventions priming imagination of the future decrease willingness to violate moral norms,[10] and (4) experimental inhibitions of mental time-travel (via transcranial magnetic stimulation) result not only in greater impulsivity but also greater egocentricity, selfishness, deficits in other-perspective-taking (OPT), and less-prosocial behavior.[11] Finally, nearly all nonhuman animals—who we do not treat as morally responsible agents—appear to lack robust mental time-travel capacities.[12] Although evidence[13] suggests that that a few other species—other hominids (great apes) and corvids (crows)—may have some mental time-travel capacities, their ability to simulate the past and future appears limited to hours, whereas human beings can simulate events years or decades in the past or future.

The apparently unique human capacity to simulate many different possible pasts and futures appears central to our vastly greater problem-solving capacities compared to nonhuman animals, such as our ability to create advanced technology (by enabling us to imagine many different possible solutions and outcomes to any particular problem). Further, when combined with OPT—the ability to simulate others' perspectives—mental time-travel also enables us to simulate how our past actions have affected others and how our future actions may affect others: capacities that have been observed to improve moral behavior when stimulated[14] and degrade moral behavior when inhibited,[15] and which are severely compromised in psychopaths.[16]

Mental time-travel also appears to be central to prudence. Mentally simulating the past enables us to reflect on and learn from past mistakes. Conversely, simulating different possible futures enables us to better appreciate the subjective value[17] and probability of different potential outcomes, including the likelihood and salience of regret.[18] Finally, interventions stimulating future-directed mental time-travel improve prudential decision-making, reducing temporal-discounting[19] in ways that lead test-subjects to save more money[20] and obese individuals to reduce their energy intake.[21]

How exactly is mental time-travel involved in prudential and moral cognition? Although we must leave this for Chapters 2–4, some potential answers immediately emerge. First, mental time-travel enables us to simulate how our actions may affect ourselves (viz. prudence) and others (viz. morality). Second, mental time-travel enables us to simulate how we have regretted imprudent and immoral behavior in our past, as well as how we might regret imprudent or immoral behavior in the future. It is thus plausibly implicated in normative reasoning—both prudential and moral—about why we should behave differently than in the past and about how we should behave in the future.

2 Other-Perspective-Taking

OPT is the capacity to simulate other people's perspectives—their beliefs, feelings, and experiences—as though they are one's own.[22] OPT is implicated in prudential decision-making as 'an essential strategy in intertemporal choices', resulting in reduced temporal discounting (viz. greater focus on long-term benefit).[23] It is also implicated in moral cognition, as OPT enables us to appreciate how our actions affect others from their perspective through emotional empathy.[24] Importantly, OPT and mental time-travel have been found to be neurofunctionally related. Experimental inhibitions of the right temporoparietal junction (TPJ) via transcranial magnetic stimulation have been found to simultaneously inhibit OPT and mental time-travel, inhibiting the general ability of individuals to overcome their own perspective in the present, thereby inhibiting their ability to consider or care about the perspectives of other people *and* their own future selves.[25]

How exactly is OPT implicated in prudential and moral cognition? Again, although we must leave this for Chapters 2–4, obvious candidate hypotheses emerge. First, OPT enables us to imagine how others might react to our actions, rewarding or punishing us for our behavior in the present (viz. prudence). Second, OPT enables us to empathize with others, 'imagining ourselves in their shoes' (viz. morality). As we will see in Chapter 3, I do not equate morality with empathy, but instead see *normatively rational* empathy as a component of normative moral reasoning.

3 Risk-Aversion

Human beings have a pronounced tendency toward risk-aversion, or preferring sure payments over gambles with equal or higher expected value.[26] Although people sometimes do take risks, empirical studies and experiments indicate that people have a pronounced tendency to attach substantially greater weight to avoiding negative outcomes than to obtaining potential gains, weighting the value of sure gains more heavily than moderate or high probability gains that have some prospect for loss.[27] Risk-aversion is thus linked to loss-aversion: people tend to be risk-averse *because* they tend to fear losses more than they desire gains.[28] Risk-aversion has also been argued to be prudentially rational for many reasons,[29] including pain being a more salient sensation than pleasure,[30] loss being more aversive than gain being pleasant,[31] and risk-aversion being vital to self-preservation (including preservation of economic and social status).[32] Finally, risk-aversion is implicated in moral cognition, with human subjects displaying pronounced 'moral risk-aversion', where 'people err on the side of caution to avoid imposing intolerable costs on others'.[33] Conversely, psychopaths are notoriously *non*-risk-averse (or risk-seekers), showing pronounced deficits in the ability to learn from negative outcomes from past risks[34] and the ability to use prospective regret about the future to inhibit risk-taking behavior.[35]

How does risk-aversion figure into prudential and moral cognition? Although we must again leave this for later, Chapter 2 argues that prudence normatively requires a specific form of 'moral risk-aversion' that involves worrying prospectively about the ways one might regret immoral behavior, leading prudent individuals to not want to risk immoral behavior. Chapter 3 then derives a normative moral theory and descriptive theory of moral cognition from this prudential foundation.

4 The Default Mode Network

Finally, the human brain's *Default Mode Network* (DMN)—a widely distributed neurofunctional system involved in daydreaming, mind-wandering, thinking about others, thinking about oneself, remembering the past, and planning for the future[36]—has been systematically implicated in moral and prudential cognition.

12 Outline of Behavioral Neuroscience

First, the following 12 DMN regions are systematically involved in *moral judgment* (i.e. moral belief) across a wide variety of tasks[37]:

a   *Ventromedial prefrontal cortex* (vmPFC)[38]: processes risk, uncertainty, and stimulus value (expected-benefit), in ways associated with learning from mistakes and applying moral judgments to one's own behavior,[39] as well as the expected moral value of alternatives in moral dilemmas.[40] Also associated with emotional regulation.[41] Deficits lead to lack of empathy, irresponsibility, and poor decision-making,[42] causing patients to choose immediate rewards insensitive to future consequences.[43] Also implicated in 'extinction', the process whereby previously reinforced behaviors gradually cease when reinforcement ceases.[44]

b   *Dorsomedial prefrontal cortex* (dmPFC): associated with sense of self[45] and theory of mind (understanding others' mental-states).[46]

c   TPJ: associated with sympathy and empathy via the representation of different possible perspectives on a single situation.[47] Also implicated in 'out-of-body experiences', where one's first-personal perspective occupies what is ordinarily a third-personal standpoint.[48] Also associated with mental time-travel and empathy with one's own future selves,[49] as well as processing order of events in time.[50]

   a   Includes *Wernicke's area*, associated with 'inner monologue'.[51]
   b   Includes the *angular gyrus*, which processes attention to visual features of situations,[52] mediates episodic memory retrieval to infer the intentions of other people,[53] and is associated with representing the mental states of individuals in cartoons and stories.[54]

d   *Middle temporal gyrus* (MTG): associated with contemplating distance from oneself, facial-recognition, and word-meaning while reading.[55]

e   *Superior temporal sulcus* (STC): associated with social perception, including where others are gazing (viz. joint attention) and direction of others' emotions.[56]

f   *Middle occipital gyrus* (MOG): contains topographical maps of external world and engages in spatial processing.[57]

g   *Temporal pole* (TP): associated with conceptual knowledge[58]; semantic memory of objects, people, words, and facts[59]; facial recognition, theory of mind, and visceral emotional responses.[60]

Outline of Behavioral Neuroscience 13

h *Fusiform gyrus* (FG): facial and visual-word recognition.[61]
i *Inferior temporal gyrus* (ITG): object recognition[62] and facial recognition.[63]
j *Precuneus* (PC): a neural correlate of consciousness[64] involved in self-awareness,[65] episodic memory[66] (including past events affecting oneself),[67] and visual imagery and attention, particularly representing other people's points-of-view[68] (activation of which has been implicated in empathy and forgiveness).[69]

Many of these same regions are also implicated in *moral sensitivity*, the capacity to monitor and recognize morally salient details of a given situation.[70] However, moral sensitivity has also been found to involve the following five additional DMN regions across a wide variety of tasks:

k *Cingulate gyrus* (CG): emotional processing, memory, and learning, particularly linking outcomes to motivational behavior.[71]
l *Orbitofrontal cortex* (OFC): processes cross-temporal (i.e. diachronic) contingencies and representation of the relative subjective value of outcomes.[72] Also associated with processing reward and punishment, learning from counterfactual prediction errors,[73] reversing behavior,[74] autonomic nervous system regulation[75] (e.g. heartbeat and sexual arousal), and behavioral inhibition related to moral behavior.[76] Damage produces extreme changes in personality, most famously associated with Phineas Gage, who dramatically transformed from a broadly prudent and moral individual into a reckless person unable to resist morally base impulses.[77]
m *Lingual gyrus* (LG): visual processing (including memories and dreams),[78] particularly memories of parts of faces.[79]
n *Cuneus:* visual processing and behavioral inhibition,[80] but also pathological gambling in those with high activity in the dorsal visual processing system.[81]
o *Amygdala*: long-term emotional-memory consolidation, specifically fear conditioning,[82] but also positive (reward-based) conditioning.[83] Also involved in decision-making involving fear, anger, sadness, and anxiety,[84] and in using emotional valence (positive or negative) to motivate behavior more generally.[85]

How are all of these DMN regions and associated capacities involved in prudential and moral cognition? Although Chapters 2 and 3 provide a unified theory of prudential and moral cognition involving all of the above capacities, notice for now that many of the above capacities are intuitively central to moral and prudential cognition. Understanding potential future consequences, adopting other people's perspectives, and engaging in emotional learning (including fear-conditioning to avoid past prudential and moral mistakes)—capacities associated with DMN regions—all seem crucial both for long-term planning (viz. prudence) and for understanding and caring about other people's perspectives and interests (viz. morality). This is underscored by empirical findings that psychopaths appear to take imprudent risks and violate moral norms due to compromised abilities to learn from social punishment (viz. fear conditioning),[86] vividly imagine potential consequences through mental time-travel,[87] use prospective regret to inhibit their behavior,[88] understand facial expressions,[89] and engage in empathetic OPT[90]—all capacities associated with the DMN. Further, particular DMN regions have been found to have pervasive effects on prudential and moral behavior. Stimulation of the TPJ has been found to induce pro-social (moral) action.[91] Conversely, TPJ inhibition has been observed to simultaneously degrade prudential and moral performance.[92] Finally, larger TPJs are linked to altruism[93] and better-interconnected TPJs linked to reduced intergroup bias.[94]

While many of these brain regions and capacities appear to be central to prudential and moral cognition, these findings nevertheless fit poorly with dominant philosophical approaches to ethics and moral psychology. First, meta-ethicists do not normally understand moral beliefs as having anything essential to do with risk-aversion, mental time-travel, or episodic memory of the past, let alone self-awareness, visual processing, representation of cartoons or stories, or extinction of past behaviors. Instead, meta-ethicists tend to understand moral beliefs in either broadly representational or non-representational terms (viz. cognitivism vs. non-cognitivism).[95] Further, with very few exceptions,[96] mainstream theories have not aimed to reduce moral cognition or sensitivity to complex interactions between mental-time-travel, risk-aversion, and dozens of other functions listed above. Instead, normative moral theorists and moral psychologists typically understand moral cognition in terms of beliefs and desires,[97] sensitivity to moral reasons,[98] constitutive features of agency,[99] moral principles,[100] transcendental freedom,[101] intuitions,[102] virtues,[103] reasonability,[104] or emotions such as sympathy and empathy.[105] As Chapter 4 explains, it may be possible to retrofit these frameworks to the above neuroscience.

However, or so Chapter 4 argues, this book's theory provides a more compelling normative and descriptive explanation of the behavioral neuroscience than these more traditional views.

5 Conclusion

As we will see further in Chapter 4, the behavioral neuroscience summarized above raises two questions: (1) the *normative* question of why the brain regions and capacities listed should be involved in prudential and moral cognition, and (2) the *descriptive* question of how various mental capacities, dispositions, and brain regions actually function in moral and prudential cognition. Chapters 2 and 3 will now outline a novel normative and descriptive theory of prudence and morality. Chapter 4 will then argue that the theory proposed answers the above questions better than existing alternatives.

Notes

1. Suddendorf and Corballis (2007).
2. Kennett and Matthews (2009), Levy (2007).
3. Kennett and Matthews (2009), Levy (2007), Suddendorf and Corballis (2007).
4. Kennett and Matthews (2009), Levy (2007).
5. Blair (2003), Casey *et al.* (2008), Giedd *et al.* (1999), Kennett and Matthews (2009), Levy (2007), Stuss *et al.* (1992), Weber *et al.* (2008), Yang and Raine (2009).
6. Baskin-Sommers *et al.* (2016), Hare (1999), Hart and Dempster (1997), Litton (2008), Moffit (1993), Moffit *et al.* (2011), Shoemaker (2011).
7. Van Gelder *et al.* (2013).
8. Hosking *et al.* (2017).
9. Hershfield *et al.* (2012).
10. Van Gelder *et al.* (2013).
11. Soutschek *et al.* (2016).
12. Suddendorf and Corballis (2007).
13. Kabadayi and Osvath (2017).
14. Van Gelder *et al.* (2013).
15. Soustchek *et al.* (2016).
16. Baskin-Sommers *et al.* (2016), Decety *et al.* (2013), Kennett and Matthews (2009), Levy (2007).
17. McCoy *et al.* (2019), Paul (2015a, 2015b).
18. Baskin-Sommers *et al.* (2016).
19. Pronin *et al.* (2008).
20. Ersner-Hershfield *et al.* (2009a, 2009b), Hershfield *et al.* (2011).
21. Daniel *et al.* (2013).
22. Galinsky *et al.* (2008).
23. Viganò (2017): 219–21. Cf. Benoit *et al.* (2011), Daniel *et al.* (2013), Peters and Büchel (2010).

24 Arvan (2016): Chapter 4, Singer and Lamm (2009), Singer and Tusche (2014), Viganò (2017): 219, 227.
25 Santiesteban *et al.* (2012), Soutschek *et al.* (2016).
26 Bliss and Panigirtzoglou (2004), Kahneman and Tversky (1984), Hartley *et al.* (2014), Tom *et al.* (2007).
27 Baumeister *et al.* (2001), Ito *et al.* (1998), Kahneman and Tversky (1979).
28 Kahneman and Tversky (1984), Viganò (2017): 221–2.
29 Menegatti (2014).
30 Viganò (2017): 219, who cites Smith [1759]: I.iii.1.8: 45; III.2.15: 121.
31 Kahneman and Tversky (1979).
32 Viganò (2017): 221–2.
33 Crockett *et al.* (2015): 1856.
34 Birbaumer *et al.* (2005).
35 Baskin-Sommers *et al.* (2016).
36 Buckner and Carroll (2007), Buckner *et al.* (2008).
37 Han (2017). See also Sommer *et al.* (2014).
38 The vmPFC is also involved in gender stereotyping (Milne and Grafman 2001).
39 Fellows and Farah (2007).
40 Shenhav and Greene (2010, 2014).
41 Koenigs *et al.* (2007).
42 Motzkin *et al.* (2011).
43 Bechara *et al.* (2000).
44 Milad *et al.* (2005).
45 Gusnard *et al.* (2001).
46 Isoda and Nirotake (2013).
47 Decety and Lamm (2007).
48 Blanke *et al.* (2005).
49 Soutschek *et al.* (2016).
50 Davis *et al.* (2009).
51 Shergill *et al.* (2001). Wernicke's area is also associated with processing word-meaning (Harpaz *et al.* 2009).
52 Seghier (2013).
53 Ibid.
54 Gallagher *et al.* (2000).
55 Acheson and Hagoort (2013).
56 Campbell *et al.* (1990). The STC is also associated with hearing human voices, motor outputs, and phonology (Belin *et al.* 2000).
57 Renier *et al.* (2010).
58 Lambon Ralph *et al.* (2008).
59 Bonner and Price (2013).
60 Olson *et al.* (2007).
61 George *et al.* (1999), McCandliss *et al.* (2003), McCarthy *et al.* (1997). The fusiform gyrus is also associated with color-processing and synesthesia (Hubbard and Ramachandran 2005).
62 Spiridon *et al.* (2006).
63 Meadows (1974), Purves *et al.* (2001): 622.
64 Vogt and Laureys (2005).
65 Kjaer *et al.* (2002).
66 Lundstrom *et al.* (2003).

67 Lou et al. (2004).
68 Vogeley et al. (2004).
69 Farrow et al. (2001).
70 Han (2017): 98.
71 Hayden and Platt (2010)
72 Fettes et al. (2017).
73 Kringelbach and Rolls (2004).
74 Walton et al. (2010).
75 Barbas (2007).
76 Fuster (2001).
77 Damasio et al. (1994), Harlow [1848].
78 Bogousslavsky et al. (1987).
79 McCarthy et al. (1999).
80 Haldane et al. (2008).
81 Crockford et al. (2005).
82 Maren (1999).
83 Paton et al. (2006).
84 Amunts et al. (2005).
85 Nieh et al. (2013).
86 Birbaumer et al. (2005).
87 Hosking et al. (2017).
88 Soutschek et al. (2016).
89 Marsh and Blair (2008).
90 Decety et al. (2013).
91 Santiesteban et al. (2012).
92 Soutschek et al. (2016).
93 Morishima et al. (2012).
94 Baumgartner et al. (2015).
95 See Van Roojen (2016).
96 Arvan (2016), Viganò (2017).
97 Hume [1751], Sinhababu (2017), Smith (1994).
98 Parfit (2011), Scanlon (1998, 2014).
99 Korsgaard (2008, 2009).
100 May (2018).
101 Kant [1785].
102 Audi (2005), Ross [1930].
103 Hursthouse (1999), Swanton (2001).
104 Sterba (2013).
105 Haidt (2001), Hume [1751], Slote (2009).

References

Acheson, D.J. & Hagoort, P. (2013). Stimulating the Brain's Language Network: Syntactic Ambiguity Resolution after TMS to the Inferior Frontal Gyrus and Middle Temporal Gyrus. *Journal of Cognitive Neuroscience*, 25(10), 1664–77.

Amunts, K., Kedo, O., Kindler, M., Pieperhoff, P., Mohlberg, H., Shah, N. J., ... Zilles, K. (2005). Cytoarchitectonic Mapping of the Human Amygdala, Hippocampal Region and Entorhinal Cortex: Intersubject

Variability and Probability Maps. *Anatomy and Embryology, 210*(5–6), 343–52.
Arvan, M. (2016). *Rightness as Fairness: A Moral and Political Theory.* New York: Palgrave MacMillan.
Audi, R. (2015). Intuition and Its Place in Ethics. *Journal of the American Philosophical Association, 1*(1), 57–77.
Barbas, H. (2007). Flow of Information for Emotions through Temporal and Orbitofrontal Pathways. *Journal of Anatomy, 211*(2), 237–49.
Baskin-Sommers, A., Stuppy-Sullivan, A.M., & Buckholtz, J.W. (2016). Psychopathic Individuals Exhibit But Do Not Avoid Regret during Counterfactual Decision Making. *Proceedings of the National Academy of Sciences, 113*(50), 14438–43.
Baumgartner, T., Nash, K., Hill, C., & Knoch, D. (2015). Neuroanatomy of Intergroup Bias: A White Matter Microstructure Study of Individual Differences. *NeuroImage, 122*, 345–54.
Baumeister, R.F., Bratslavsky, E., Finkenauer, C., & Vohs, K.D. (2001). Bad is Stronger than Good. *Review of General Psychology, 5*(4), 323–70.
Bechara, A., Tranel, D., & Damasio, H. (2000). Characterization of the Decision-Making Deficit of Patients with Ventromedial Prefrontal Cortex Lesions. *Brain, 123*(11), 2189–202.
Belin, P., Zatorre, R.J., Lafaille, P., Ahad, P., & Pike, B. (2000). Voice-Selective Areas in Human Auditory Cortex. *Nature, 403*(6767), 309–12.
Benoit, R.G., Gilbert, S.J., & Burgess, P.W. (2011). A Neural Mechanism Mediating the Impact of Episodic Prospection on Farsighted Decisions. *The Journal of Neuroscience, 31*(18), 6771–9.
Birbaumer, N., Veit, R., Lotze, M., Erb, M., Hermann, C., Grodd, W., & Flor, H. (2005). Deficient Fear Conditioning in Psychopathy: A Functional Magnetic Resonance Imaging Study. *Archives of General Psychiatry, 62*(7), 799–805.
Blair, R.J.R. (2003). Neurobiological Basis of Psychopathy. *The British Journal of Psychiatry, 182*(1), 5–7.
Blanke, O., Mohr, C., Michel, C. M., Pascual-Leone, A., Brugger, P., Seeck, M., ... Thut, G. (2005). Linking Out-of-Body Experience and Self Processing to Mental Own-Body Imagery at the Temporoparietal Junction. *Journal of Neuroscience, 25*(3), 550–7.
Bliss, R.R. & Panigirtzoglou, N. (2004). Option-implied Risk Aversion Estimates. *The Journal of Finance, 59*(1), 407–46.
Bogousslavsky, J., Miklossy, J., Deruaz, J.P., Assal, G., & Regli, F. (1987). Lingual and Fusiform Gyri in Visual Processing: A Clinico-Pathologic Study of Superior Altitudinal Hemianopia. *Journal of Neurology, Neurosurgery & Psychiatry, 50*(5), 607–14.
Bonner, M.F. & Price, A.R. (2013). Where is the Anterior Temporal Lobe and What Does it Do? *Journal of Neuroscience, 33*(10), 4213–5.
Buckner, R.L., Andrews-Hanna, J.R., & Schacter, D.L. (2008). The Brain's Default Network: Anatomy, Function, and Relevance to Disease. *Annals of the New York Academy of Sciences, 1124*, 1–38.

Buckner, R.L. & Carroll, D.C. (2007). Self-Projection and the Brain. *Trends in Cognitive Sciences*, *11*(2), 49–57.

Campbell, R., Heywood, C.A., Cowey, A., Regard, M., & Landis, T. (1990). Sensitivity to Eye Gaze in Prosopagnosic Patients and Monkeys with Superior Temporal Sulcus Ablation. *Neuropsychologia*, *28*(11), 1123–42.

Casey, B.J., Jones, R.M., & Hare, T.A. (2008). The Adolescent Brain. *Annals of the New York Academy of Sciences*, *1124*, 111–26.

Crockett, M.J., Siegel, J.Z., Kurth-Nelson, Z., Ousdal, O.T., Story, G., Frieband, C., ... Dolan, R.J. (2015). Dissociable Effects of Serotonin and Dopamine on the Valuation of Harm in Moral Decision Making. *Current Biology*, *25*(14), 1852–9.

Crockford, D.N., Goodyear, B., Edwards, J., Quickfall, J., & el-Guebaly, N. (2005). Cue-Induced Brain Activity in Pathological Gamblers. *Biological Psychiatry*, *58*(10), 787–95.

Damasio, H., Grabowski, T., Frank, R., Galaburda, A.M., & Damasio, A.R. (1994). The Return of Phineas Gage: Clues about the Brain from the Skull of a Famous Patient. *Science*, *264*(5162), 1102–5.

Daniel, T.O., Stanton, C.M., & Epstein, L.H. (2013). The Future is Now: Comparing the Effect of Episodic Future Thinking on Impulsivity in Lean and Obese Individuals. *Appetite*, *71*, 120–5.

Davis, B., Christie, J., & Rorden, C. (2009). Temporal Order Judgments Activate Temporal Parietal Junction. *Journal of Neuroscience*, *29*(10), 3182–8.

Decety, J. & Lamm, C. (2007). The Role of the Right Temporoparietal Junction in Social Interaction: How Low-Level Computational Processes Contribute to Meta-Cognition. *The Neuroscientist*, *13*(6), 580–93.

Ersner-Hershfield, H., Garton, M.T., Ballard, K., Samanez-Larkin, G.R., & Knutson, B. (2009a). Don't Stop Thinking about Tomorrow: Individual Differences in Future Self-continuity Account for Saving. *Judgment and Decision Making*, *4*, 280–6.

Ersner-Hershfield, H., Wimmer, G.E., & Knutson, B. (2009b). Saving for the Future Self: Neural Measures of Future Self-Continuity Predict Temporal Discounting. *Social Cognitive and Affective Neuroscience*, *4*(1), 85–92.

Farrow, T.F., Ying Zheng, Y., Wilkinson, I.D., Spence, S.A., Deakin, J.F., Tarrier, N., ... Woodruff, P.W. (2001). Investigating the Functional Anatomy of Empathy and Forgiveness. *Neuroreport*, *12*(11), 2433–8.

Fellows, L.K. & Farah, M.J. (2007). The Role of Ventromedial Prefrontal Cortex in Decision Making: Judgment under Uncertainty or Judgment Per Se? *Cerebral Cortex*, *17*(11), 2669–74.

Fettes, P., Schulze, L., & Downar, J. (2017). Cortico-Striatal-Thalamic Loop Circuits of the Orbitofrontal Cortex: Promising Therapeutic Targets in Psychiatric Illness. *Frontiers in Systems Neuroscience*, *11*, 1–23.

Fuster, J.M. (2001). The Prefrontal Cortex—An Update: Time is of the Essence. *Neuron*, *30*(2), 319–33.

Galinsky, A.D., Maddux, W.W., Gilin, D., & White, J.B. (2008). Why It Pays to get Inside the Head of Your Opponent: The Differential Effects of Perspective Taking and Empathy in Negotiations. *Psychological Science*, *19*(4), 378–84.

Gallagher, H.L., Happé, F., Brunswick, N., Fletcher, P.C., Frith, U., & Frith, C.D. (2000). Reading the Mind in Cartoons and Stories: An fMRI Study of 'Theory of Mind' in Verbal and Nonverbal Tasks. *Neuropsychologia*, *38*(1), 11–21.

George, N., Dolan, R.J., Fink, G.R., Baylis, G.C., Russell, C., & Driver, J. (1999). Contrast Polarity and Face Recognition in the Human Fusiform Gyrus. *Nature Neuroscience*, *2*(6), 574–80.

Giedd, J.N., Blumenthal, J., & Jeffries, N.O. (1999). Brain Development during Childhood and Adolescence: A Longitudinal MRI Study. *Nature Neuroscience*, *2*(10), 861–3.

Gusnard, D.A., Akbudak, E., Shulman, G.L., & Raichle, M.E. (2001). Medial Prefrontal Cortex and Self-Referential Mental Activity: Relation to a Default Mode of Brain Function. *Proceedings of the National Academy of Sciences*, *98*(7), 4259–64.

Haidt, J. (2001). The Emotional Dog and Its Rational Tail: A Social Intuitionist Approach to Moral Judgment. *Psychological Review*, *108*(4), 814–34.

Haldane, M., Cunningham, G., Androutsos, C., & Frangou, S. (2008). Structural Brain Correlates of Response Inhibition in Bipolar Disorder I. *Journal of Psychopharmacology*, *22*(2), 138–43.

Han, H. (2017). Neural Correlates of Moral Sensitivity and Moral Judgment Associated with Brain Circuitries of Selfhood: A Meta-Analysis. *Journal of Moral Education*, *46*(2), 97–113.

Hare, R.D. (1999). *The Hare Psychopathy Checklist-Revised: PLC-R*. Toronto: Multi-Health Systems.

Harlow, J.M. [1848]. Passage of an Iron Rod through the Head. Reprinted *The Journal of Neuropsychiatry and Clinical Neurosciences*, *11*(2), 1999, 281–3.

Harpaz, Y., Levkovitz, Y., & Lavidor, M. (2009). Lexical Ambiguity Resolution in Wernicke's Area and Its Right Homologue. *Cortex*, *45*(9), 1097–103.

Hart, S.D. & Dempster, R.J. (1997). Impulsivity and Psychopathy. In C.D. Webster & M.A. Jackson (eds.), *Impulsivity: Theory, Assessment, and Treatment*. New York: The Guilford Press, 212–32.

Hartley, R., Lanot, G., & Walker, I. (2014). Who Really Wants to be a Millionaire? Estimates of Risk Aversion from Gameshow Data. *Journal of Applied Econometrics*, *29*(6), 861–79.

Hayden, B.Y. & Platt, M.L. (2010). Neurons in Anterior Cingulate Cortex Multiplex Information about Reward and Action. *Journal of Neuroscience*, *30*(9), 3339–46.

Hershfield, H.E., Cohen, T.R., & Thompson, L. (2012). Short Horizons and Tempting Situations: Lack of Continuity to our Future Selves Leads to

Unethical Decision Making and Behavior. *Organizational Behavior and Human Decision Processes*, *117*, 298–310.

Hershfield, H.E., Goldstein, D.G., Sharpe, W.F., Fox, J., Yeykelis, L., Carstensen, L.L, & Bailenson, J.N. (2011). Increasing Saving Behavior through Age-Progressed Renderings of the Future Self. *Journal of Marketing Research*, *48*, S23–S37.

Hosking, J.G., Kastman, E.K., Dorfman, H.M., Samanez-Larkin, G.R., Baskin-Sommers, A., Kiehl, K.A., ... Buckholtz, J. W. (2017). Disrupted Prefrontal Regulation of Striatal Subjective Value Signals in Psychopathy. *Neuron*, *95*(1), 221–31.

Hubbard, E.M. & Ramachandran, V.S. (2005). Neurocognitive Mechanisms of Synesthesia. *Neuron*, *48*(3), 509–20.

Hume, D. [1751]. *An Enquiry Concerning the Principles of Morals*. Indianapolis: Hackett Publishing Company, 1983.

Hursthouse, R. (1999). *On Virtue Ethics*. Oxford: Oxford University Press.

Isoda, M. & Noritake, A. (2013). What Makes the Dorsomedial Frontal Cortex Active During Reading the Mental States of Others? *Frontiers in Neuroscience*, *7*(232), 1–14.

Ito, T.A., Larsen, J.T., Smith, N.K., & Cacioppo, J.T. (1998). Negative Information Weighs More Heavily on the Brain: The Negativity Bias in Evaluative Categorizations. *Journal of Personality and Social Psychology*, *75*(4), 887–900.

Kabadayi, C. & Osvath, M. (2017). Ravens Parallel Great Apes in Flexible Planning for Tool-Use and Bartering. *Science*, *357*(6347), 202–4.

Kahneman, D. & Tversky, A. (1984). Choices, Values, and Frames. *American Psychologist*, *39*(4), 341–50.

——— (1979). Prospect Theory: An Analysis of Decision under Risk. *Econometrica*, *4*, 263–91.

Kant, I. [1785]. Groundwork of the Metaphysics of Morals. In M.J. Gregor (ed.), *The Cambridge Edition of the Works of Immanuel Kant: Practical Philosophy*. Cambridge: Cambridge University Press, 1996, 38–108.

Kennett, J. & Matthews, S. (2009). Mental Time Travel, Agency and Responsibility. In M. Broome & L. Bortolotti (eds.), *Psychiatry as Cognitive Neuroscience: Philosophical Perspectives*. Oxford: Oxford University Press, 327–50.

Kjaer, T.W., Nowak, M., & Lou, H.C. (2002). Reflective Self-Awareness and Conscious States: PET Evidence for a Common Midline Parietofrontal Core. *Neuroimage*, *17*(2), 1080–6.

Koenigs, M., Young, L., Adolphs, R., Tranel, D., Cushman, F., Hauser, M., & Damasio, A. (2007). Damage to the Prefrontal Cortex Increases Utilitarian Moral Judgements. *Nature*, *446*(7138), 908–11.

Korsgaard, C.M. (2009). *Self-Constitution: Agency, Identity, and Integrity*. Oxford: Oxford University Press.

——— (2008). *The Constitution of Agency*. Oxford: Oxford University Press.

Kringelbach, M.L. & Rolls, E.T. (2004). The Functional Neuroanatomy of the Human Orbitofrontal Cortex: Evidence from Neuroimaging and Neuropsychology. *Progress in Neurobiology*, *72*(5), 341–72.

Lambon Ralph, M.A., Pobric, G., & Jefferies, E. (2008). Conceptual Knowledge is Underpinned by the Temporal Pole Bilaterally: Convergent Evidence from rTMS. *Cerebral Cortex*, *19*(4), 832–8.

Levy, N. (2007). The Responsibility of the Psychopath Revisited. *Philosophy, Psychiatry, and Psychology*, *14*(2), 129–38.

Litton, P. (2008). Responsibility Status of the Psychopath: On Moral Reasoning and Rational Self-Governance. *Rutgers Law Journal*, *39*(349), 350–92.

Lou, H.C., Luber, B., Crupain, M., Keenan, J.P., Nowak, M., Kjaer, … Lisanby, S.H. (2004). Parietal Cortex and Representation of the Mental Self. *Proceedings of the National Academy of Sciences*, *101*(17), 6827–32.

Lundstrom, B.N., Petersson, K.M., Andersson, J., Johansson, M., Fransson, P., & Ingvar, M. (2003). Isolating the Retrieval of Imagined Pictures during Episodic Memory: Activation of the Left Precuneus and Left Prefrontal Cortex. *Neuroimage*, *20*(4), 1934–43.

Maren, S. (1999). Long-Term Potentiation in the Amygdala: A Mechanism for Emotional Learning and Memory. *Trends in Neurosciences*, *22*(12), 561–7.

Marsh, A.A. & Blair, R.J.R. (2008). Deficits in Facial Affect Recognition Among Antisocial Populations: A Meta-Analysis. *Neuroscience & Biobehavioral Reviews*, *32*(3), 454–65.

May, J. (2018). *Regard for Reason in the Moral Mind*. Oxford: Oxford University Press.

McCandliss, B.D., Cohen, L., & Dehaene, S. (2003). The Visual Word Form Area: Expertise for Reading in the Fusiform Gyrus. *Trends in Cognitive Sciences*, *7*(7), 293–9.

McCarthy, G., Puce, A., Belger, A., & Allison, T. (1999). Electrophysiological Studies of Human Face Perception. II: Response Properties of Face-Specific Potentials Generated in Occipitotemporal Cortex. *Cerebral Cortex*, *9*(5), 431–44.

McCarthy, G., Puce, A., Gore, J.C., & Allison, T. (1997). Face-Specific Processing in the Human Fusiform Gyrus. *Journal of Cognitive Neuroscience*, *9*(5), 605–10.

McCoy, J., Paul, L.A., & Ullman, T. (2019). Modal Prospection. In A. Goldman & B. McLaughlin (eds.), *Metaphysics and Cognitive Science*. New York: Oxford University Press, 235–67.

Meadows, J.C. (1974). The Anatomical Basis of Orosopagnosia. *Journal of Neurology, Neurosurgery & Psychiatry*, *37*(5), 489–501.

Menegatti, M. (2014). New Results on the Relationship among Risk Aversion, Prudence and Temperance. *European Journal of Operational Research*, *232*(3), 613–7.

Milad, M.R., Quinn, B.T., Pitman, R.K., Orr, S.P., Fischl, B., & Rauch, S.L. (2005). Thickness of Ventromedial Prefrontal Cortex in Humans is Correlated with Extinction Memory. *Proceedings of the National Academy of Sciences*, *102*(30), 10706–11.

Milne, E. & Grafman, J. (2001). Ventromedial Prefrontal Cortex Lesions in Humans Eliminate Implicit Gender Stereotyping. *Journal of Neuroscience*, *21*(12), RC150–RC156.

Moffitt, T.E. (1993). Adolescence-limited and Life-course Persistent Antisocial Behavior: A Developmental Taxonomy. *Psychological Review*, *100*, 674–701.

Moffitt, T.E., Arseneault, L., Belsky, D., Dickson, N., Hancox, R.J., Harrington, H., ... Caspi, A. (2011). A Gradient of Childhood Self-control Predicts Health, Wealth, and Public Safety. *Proceedings of the National Academy of Sciences*, *108*(7), 2693–8.

Morishima, Y., Schunk, D., Bruhin, A., Ruff, C.C., & Fehr, E. (2012). Linking Brain Structure and Activation in Temporoparietal Junction to Explain the Neurobiology of Human Altruism. *Neuron*, *75*(1), 73–9.

Motzkin, J.C., Newman, J.P., Kiehl, K.A., & Koenigs, M. (2011). Reduced Prefrontal Connectivity in Psychopathy. *Journal of Neuroscience*, *31*(48), 17348–57.

Nieh, E.H., Kim, S.Y., Namburi, P., & Tye, K.M. (2013). Optogenetic Dissection of Neural Circuits Underlying Emotional Valence and Motivated Behaviors. *Brain Research*, *1511*, 73–92.

Olson, I.R., Plotzker, A., & Ezzyat, Y. (2007). The Enigmatic Temporal Pole: A Review of Findings on Social and Emotional Processing. *Brain*, *130*(7), 1718–31.

Parfit, D. (2011). *On What Matters, Vols. 1&2*. Oxford: Oxford University Press.

Paton, J.J., Belova, M.A., Morrison, S.E., & Salzman, C.D. (2006). The Primate Amygdala Represents the Positive and Negative Value of Visual Stimuli during Learning. *Nature*, *439*(7078), 865–70.

Paul, L.A. (2015a). *Transformative Experience*. Oxford: Oxford University Press.

——— (2015b). What You Can't Expect When You're Expecting. *Res Philosophica*, *92*(2), 1–23.

Peters, J. & Büchel, C. (2010). Episodic Future Thinking Reduces Reward Delay Discounting Through an Enhancement of Prefrontal-Mediotemporal Interactions. *Neuron*, *66*(1), 138–48.

Pronin, E., Olivola, C.Y., & Kennedy, K.A. (2008). Doing Unto Future Selves as You Would Do Unto Others: Psychological Distance and Decision Making. *Personality and Social Psychology Bulletin*, *34*(2), 224–36.

Purves D., Augustine G.J., Fitzpatrick D., Hall, W.C., LaMantia, A., McNamara, J.O., & Williams, S.M. [eds.] (2001). *Neuroscience*. 2nd edition. Sunderland MA: Sinauer Associates.

Renier, L.A., Anurova, I., De Volder, A.G., Carlson, S., VanMeter, J., & Rauschecker, J.P. (2010). Preserved Functional Specialization for Spatial Processing in the Middle Occipital Gyrus of the Early Blind. *Neuron*, *68*(1), 138–48.

Ross, W.D. [1930]. *The Right and the Good.* Oxford: Oxford University Press, 2002.

Santiesteban, I., Banissy, M.J., Catmur, C., & Bird, G. (2012). Enhancing Social Ability by Stimulating Right Temporoparietal Junction. *Current Biology, 22*(23), 2274–7.

Scanlon, T.M. (2014). *Being Realistic About Reasons.* Oxford: Oxford University Press.

——— (1998). *What We Owe to Each Other.* Cambridge, MA: Harvard University Press.

Seghier, M.L. (2013). The Angular Gyrus: Multiple Functions and Multiple Subdivisions. *The Neuroscientist, 19*(1), 43–61.

Shenhav, A. & Greene, J.D. (2010). Moral Judgments Recruit Domain-general Valuation Mechanisms to Integrate Representations of Probability and Magnitude. *Neuron, 67*(4), 667–77.

Shenhav, A. & Greene, J D. (2014). Integrative Moral Judgment: Dissociating the Roles of the Amygdala and Ventromedial Prefrontal Cortex. *Journal of Neuroscience, 34*(13), 4741–9.

Shergill, S.S., Bullmore, E.T., Brammer, M.J., Williams, S.C.R., Murray, R.M., & McGuire, P.K. (2001). A Functional Study of Auditory Verbal Imagery. *Psychological Medicine, 31*(2), 241–53.

Shoemaker, D.W. (2011). Psychopathy, Responsibility, and the Moral/Conventional Distinction. *Southern Journal of Philosophy, 49*(s1), 99–124.

Singer, T. & Lamm, C. (2009). The Social Neuroscience of Empathy. *Annals of the New York Academy of Sciences, 1156*, 81–96.

Singer, T. & Tusche. A. (2014). Understanding Others: Brain Mechanisms of Theory of Mind and Empathy. In E. Fehr (ed.), *Neuroeconomics: Decision Making and the Brain,* 2nd edition. P.W. Glimcher, London: Academic Press, 513–32.

Sinhababu, N. (2017). *Humean Nature.* Oxford: Oxford University Press.

Slote, M. (2009). *Moral Sentimentalism.* Oxford: Oxford University Press.

Smith, A. [1759]. *The Theory of Moral Sentiments,* D.D. Raphael and A.L. Macfie (eds.), *Vol. I of the Glasgow Edition of the Works and Correspondence of Adam Smith.* Indianapolis: Liberty Fund, 1982.

Smith, M. (1994). *The Moral Problem.* Malden: Wiley-Blackwell.

Sommer, M., Meinhardt, J., Rothmayr, C., Döhnel, K., Hajak, G., Rupprecht, R., & Sodian, B. (2014). Me or You? Neural Correlates of Moral Reasoning in Everyday Conflict Situations in Adolescents and Adults. *Social Neuroscience, 9*(5), 452–70.

Soutschek, A., Ruff, C. C., Strombach, T., Kalenscher, T., & Tobler, P. N. (2016). Brain Stimulation Reveals Crucial Role of Overcoming Self-Centeredness in Self-Control. *Science Advances, 2*(10), e1600992.

Spiridon, M., Fischl, B., & Kanwisher, N. (2006). Location and Spatial Profile of Category-Specific Regions in Human Extrastriate Cortex. *Human Brain Mapping, 27*(1), 77–89.

Sterba, J.P. (2013). *From Rationality to Equality.* Oxford: Oxford University Press.

Stuss D.T., Gow, C.A., & Hetherington, C.R. (1992). 'No Longer Gage': Frontal Lobe Dysfunction and Emotional Changes. *Journal of Consulting and Clinical Psychology*, *60*(3), 349–59.
Suddendorf, T. & Corballis, M.C. (2007). The Evolution of Foresight: What is Mental Time Travel, and Is It Unique to Humans? *Behavioral and Brain Sciences*, *30*(3), 299–313.
Swanton, C. (2001). A Virtue Ethical Account of Right Action. *Ethics*, *112*(1), 32–52.
Tom, S.M., Fox, C.R., Trepel, C., & Poldrack, R.A. (2007). The Neural Basis of Loss Aversion in Decision-making under Risk. *Science*, 315(5811), 515–8.
Van Gelder, J.L., Hershfield, H.E., & Nordgren, L.F. (2013). Vividness of the Future Self Predicts Delinquency. *Psychological Science*, *24*(6), 974–80.
Van Roojen, M. (2016). Moral Cognitivism vs. Non-Cognitivism. In E.N. Zalta (ed.), *The Stanford Encyclopedia of Philosophy*. https://plato.stanford.edu/archives/win2016/entries/moral-cognitivism/.
Viganò, E. (2017). Adam Smith's Theory of Prudence Updated with Neuroscientific and Behavioral Evidence. *Neuroethics*, *10*(2), 215–33.
Vogeley, K., May, M., Ritzl, A., Falkai, P., Zilles, K., & Fink, G.R. (2004). Neural Correlates of First-Person Perspective as One Constituent of Human Self-Consciousness. *Journal of Cognitive Neuroscience*, *16*(5), 817–27.
Vogt, B.A. & Laureys, S. (2005). Posterior Cingulate, Precuneal and Retrosplenial Cortices: Cytology and Components of the Neural Network Correlates of Consciousness. *Progress in Brain Research*, *150*, 205–17.
Walton, M.E., Behrens, T.E., Buckley, M.J., Rudebeck, P.H., & Rushworth, M.F. (2010). Separable Learning Systems in the Macaque Brain and the Role of Orbitofrontal Cortex in Contingent Learning. *Neuron*, *65*(6), 927–39.
Weber, S., Habel, U., Amunts, K., & Schnieder, F. (2008). Structural Brain Abnormalities in Psychopaths—A Review, *Behavioral Sciences & the Law*, *26*(1), 7–28.
Yang, Y. & Raine, A. (2009). Prefrontal Structural and Functional Brain Imaging Findings in Antisocial, Violent, and Psychopathic Individuals: A Meta-analysis. *Psychiatry Research*, *174*(2), 81–8.

2 Outline of a Theory of Prudence

There are many theories of normative rationality—that is, theories of how agents rationally ought to act—including Kantian theories of categorical rationality[1] and realist theories of rationality as responsivity to objective normative reasons.[2] However, the dominant conception of rationality in everyday life[3] and academic theorizing[4] appears to be instrumentalism, the 'means-end' view that rationality is a matter of agents adopting optimal means for achieving their ends (or goals). Notice further that this appears to be how we normally understand prudence. We say, for example, that prudent students study hard to maximize their chances of meeting their academic goals, that prudent people look both ways before crossing streets to maximize their chance of getting to the other side safely, and so on. Hence, although multiple theories of normative rationality exist, I will simply assume for theory-construction that normatively prudent behavior (henceforth 'prudence') is a matter of acting in ways that have the best-expected outcome for the agent acting, *vis-à-vis* satisfying their ends. Notice that prudence thus defined could involve what the ancient Greeks called *phronesis*, or practical wisdom and excellence of character for living an extraordinary life.[5] As we will see, this book's unified theory of prudence and morality does require forms of excellence: the development and exercise of virtues of fairness over a complete life (a kind of moral excellence), as well as excellence in the ability to judge which actions (constrained by principles of fairness) have the best-expected long-term aggregate outcomes. However, we will also see that there is a sense in which this book's theory does not demand 'excellence', at least as some laypeople and theorists understand it. For although some moral theories (such as utilitarianism) and proposed moral exemplars (e.g. Jesus Christ) appear to espouse extreme forms of altruism as 'moral excellence', this book's theory holds that true moral excellence (fairness) does not require extreme sacrifice.

In any case, assuming that prudence involves acting in instrumentally optimal ways that possess the best-expected outcomes for the acting agent, the next question is how to understand ends. Some theorists argue that ends and their value are subjective.[6] Others (hedonists) argue that ends and their value are reducible to pleasure and pain,[7] others still argue that ends and their value reduce to preference-satisfaction,[8] and so on.[9] This book cannot resolve these questions. Instead, I will simply contend that the theory of prudence that I outline below (and allow potential exceptions to in Chapter 5) is plausible given an intuitive, everyday understanding of ends and their value, with which any adequate theory of ends and their value should defeasibly cohere. I leave it to readers to judge whether this is the case.

1 Prudence as Maximizing Expected Aggregate Lifetime Utility

If prudence involves acting in ways that have the best-expected outcome for the acting agent, questions also arise about the nature and persistence of agents. Do agents like you and I literally persist over time, or are we mere 'person-stages' who exist only for a moment before new 'person-stages' come into existence?[10] As Michael Smith and I argue,[11] we do not need to settle these matters to do normative theorizing. For regardless of these metaphysical issues, throughout 'our lives'—that is, as different 'person-stages'—we tend to care about 'our' past and future. For example, at present, I wish that certain things in 'my' past had gone better than they did. I also have all kinds of hopes for 'my' future—for example, that my 'future self' sees this book to be well-received, that 'I' happily live to old age with my spouse, and so on. To be sure, empirical research shows (and commonsense recognizes) that we do not always care about our past or future 'selves'—that all too often we treat our past and future 'selves' akin to strangers.[12] Still, it is equally clear, especially in our 'cooler' moments—particularly when we reflect on the subjective experiences of 'our' past and future selves[13]—that we often care deeply about 'our' past and future. We ordinarily have standing hopes, dreams, desires, and worries about 'our' future, as well as retrospectives wishes and desires about 'our' past. Consequently, for the sake of theory-construction, we have sufficient grounds to treat agents as though they persist over time—based on our standing interests about 'our' past and future.[14]

We can use these facts to settle another important issue, at least well enough for our purposes: namely, the relevant time frame for evaluating outcomes. As Aristotle posited, our highest good (prudentially) seems to be a good life as a whole.[15] This claim appears not only widely accepted in the philosophical literature[16] but also a fair approximation of what laypeople normally care about: namely, for our *life* to go well. Consequently, for the purposes of theory-construction, it seems safe to suppose that prudence is a matter of acting in ways that have the best-expected aggregate outcomes across our lives as a whole (i.e. 'best-expected lifetime value').[17] Of course, there are many questions here, such as whether prudence permits or requires temporal favoritism, such as favoring the well-being of one's future selves over the past.[18] However, I want to set aside these matters as well. I will now argue that we can outline a compelling theory of prudence without presupposing any controversial answers to them.

2 Problems Maximizing Expected Aggregate Lifetime Utility in an Uncertain World

If we assume that prudence involves acting in whichever ways have the best-expected lifetime value, the next question concerns what it *is* for any given action to have this property. As many argue,[19] the most natural way to understand to this is 'additively', identifying prudent actions as whichever series of individual actions that, when aggregated across a full life, generate the greatest-expected *sum* of well-being. However, while this seems plausible, we nevertheless face two sets of problems in attempting to determine which actions achieve this.

One problem concerns interworld utility comparisons.[20] For an agent to determine which actions maximize their expected sum of lifetime value, it seems like the agent must be able to compare aggregate lifetime utilities of different possible lives they might have lived. However, in cases of 'big decisions'—such as whether to write a book, have a child, get married, or change careers—such comparisons seem infeasible.[21] For example, would my life be better as whole if had I never gone into academia? Might my life be better now if I abandoned my academic career in favor of another? These things seem impossible to estimate reliably. Comparing alternative lives we have never lived appears to 'require a kind and amount of knowledge which seems far out of reach (at least currently) for mere mortals like us'.[22]

Some contend that interworld comparisons are irrelevant to prudence, contending that the only thing that matters to prudence is how one feels about one's actual life.[23] Perhaps this is true, though I am skeptical. Because we cannot settle this, let us simply recognize that there seem to be *prima facie* reasons to think interworld comparisons are relevant to prudence. First, given that prudence is widely understood to be acting in ways that have the best-expected aggregate lifetime utility for the agent acting, and given that different life choices clearly can result in very different aggregate life-outcomes, alternative lives seem relevant to maximizing expected lifetime utility. Second, in everyday life, we sometimes dwell on interworld comparisons for these reasons. When our lives frustrate us, it appears common to wonder whether alternative life-choices might have been more prudent. We sometimes ask questions like, 'What if I had chosen a different career? Might my life have been happier? Indeed, might I be happier *now* if I changed careers?' Interworld comparisons, thus, seem relevant to prudence, at least in the counterfactual sense that if we *could* make such comparisons reliably, then we would be able to make choices with better expected aggregate lifetime outcomes.

In addition to problems of interworld comparisons, we also face profound difficulties evaluating the probabilities of different outcomes over a complete life. First, the future—particularly the distant future—is formidably difficult to predict. Although short-term events often go roughly how we expect, sometimes they turn out very differently and vastly transform the probabilities of future events. Consider a victim of a serious crime, such as a school shooting. Prior to the crime, the person may have regarded the likelihood of them dedicating themselves to gun-control activism to be near-zero. However, after the crime, the probability of them dedicating their life to activism may become extremely high. Although this is an extreme example, our lives routinely appear to be transformed by the unexpected—by who we meet or fall in love with, unexpected job-opportunities, illnesses, and so on. How can we reliably estimate which life-choices have the best-expected aggregate lifetime outcomes (viz. prudence) when we do not know how the probabilities of outcomes might change over our lifetime?

Second, human beings are generally poor affective-forecasters—that is, at estimating how we are likely to experience the value of different outcomes.[24] For instance, people tend to think they will be profoundly happy winning the lottery. However, empirical studies indicate only short-term spikes in subjective well-being for lottery-winners, not long-term gains.[25] More generally, we often think that particular outcomes (getting a promotion at work, etc.) will bring us satisfaction only to find the value of the outcome to be very different than expected.

Third, human beings often display preference-reversals,[26] desiring one thing prospectively in the present (e.g. winning the lottery) only to retrospectively desire the opposite later (e.g. wishing we had never won). Similarly, one may want to tell a lie in the present—and then tell it because one expects to get away with it—only to wish one hadn't when the future comes (because of getting caught or feeling guilty).

Finally, there are transformative experiences: experiences that may transform us both epistemically—giving us salient information about the subjective value of outcomes only after a choice—and personally, altering our core preferences in unpredictable ways.[27] For example, a person at one point might think their life as a whole might be happier if they remain childless, yet they may find the experience of giving birth to a child so transformative that they now value having children tremendously. Over a complete life, we plausibly undergo a variety of transformative experiences ranging from having children, to falling in love, to taking a university course that fundamentally alters one's values and career goals, and so on.

Thus, although prudence requires acting in ways that have the best-expected aggregate lifetime outcomes, we appear to face an important set of problems. Life is so uncertain, and our capacities to reliably compare and predict the value and likelihood of different outcomes over the course of our lives are so limited, that it is unclear how we can reliably determine which actions maximize expected aggregate lifetime personal utility. Various solutions to these problems have been proposed.[28] However, instead of evaluating them, I want to explore a new solution: a novel normative and descriptive theory of prudence and prudential cognition.

3 Bruckner's Prudential Original Position and Minimax Regret

There is a long tradition of thought that (a) prudence is a matter of grappling with life's immense uncertainty, and (b) morality is only prudent solution to that uncertainty. For example, the Bible repeatedly emphasizes life's unpredictability,[29] holding that moral behavior is a prudent response.[30] Similarly, the Stoics argued that life's uncertainty makes it rational to develop self-mastery over one's desires, emotions, and beliefs, holding in turn that such self-mastery constitutes morality.[31] I will now defend a new theory of prudence in this tradition.

Donald Bruckner has argued that because life is profoundly uncertain, prudence requires acting on principles that presuppose radical uncertainty.[32] Bruckner argues that this prudential requirement can be modeled by a Prudential Original Position, a hypothetical model closely akin to John Rawls' famous 'original position', but where an agent deliberates behind a veil of ignorance applied not to questions of social justice, but rather to their own life as a whole.[33] Rawls, of course, understands principles of domestic and international justice (respectively) as principles that instrumentally rational representatives of citizens in a domestic society[34] and peoples internationally[35] would agree to from an extreme position of *inter*personal uncertainty—from behind a veil of ignorance that prevents them from arbitrarily privileging themselves over any other citizen or people. Bruckner's innovative idea is that principles of prudence should be understood in a similar fashion—as principles that are instrumentally rational from a standpoint of extreme *intra*personal uncertainty, that is, from behind a veil of ignorance that withholds from an individual agent any knowledge of how their life as a whole is likely to go.

Let us assume for the sake of argument that Bruckner is correct. Which principle(s) of prudence are rational from the Prudential Original Position? Bruckner rejects several principles: intrapersonal utilitarianism (simple utility-maximization), maximin (choosing whichever action has the best worst outcome), and minimax loss (choosing whichever action minimizes the maximum shortfall experienced by any particular 'person stage'), arguing that all of these principles are implausible in test-cases.[36] There are also well-known problems with another principle for choice under extreme uncertainty: the principle of insufficient reason (treating all outcomes as equally likely)—as it seems arbitrary to treat all outcomes as equally probable when one has no evidence of this.[37] Ultimately, Bruckner argues that only minimax regret, the principle of acting in ways whose maximum possible amount of regret is lowest, gives plausible results.[38] Finally, Bruckner derives the further result that the more an agent cares about their future and past, 'the more [they] will be acting as if following the utilitarian principle of prudence [viz. utility-maximization] when actually following minimax regret'.[39]

It is not my aim to evaluate Bruckner's argument. Instead, I will now argue that two parts of his solution—minimax regret and its convergence with maximum expected aggregate value the more one cares about the past and future—cohere with a kind of 'moral risk-aversion' that prudent children, adolescents, and adults typically progressively internalize for grappling with life's uncertainty.

4 'Moral Risk-Aversion' as Maximizing Expected Aggregate Lifetime Utility

Prudence, again, is intuitively a matter of acting in whichever ways have the best-expected aggregate outcomes for one's life as a whole. Consequently, when it comes to first-order choices—that is, to deciding how to act in any given situation—prudent agents will have to weigh and aggregate different possible outcomes, in turn estimating the relative probabilities of different weighted aggregate outcomes given the ways they might change over time.[40] However, or so I will now argue, when life's immense uncertainty is combined with several empirical regularities, we can see that prudent agents should also typically internalize higher-order dispositions (beliefs and preferences) as constraints on first-order prudential deliberation. As we will now see, a set of moral dispositions constituting a kind of 'moral risk-aversion'—that is, aversion to risking the violation of moral norms—appear to be higher-order prudential dispositions of this sort: dispositions that prudent individuals typically learn are likely to make their lives as a whole go better in an otherwise uncertain world.

4.1 Depictions of the Prudence of 'Moral Risk-Aversion' in Fiction and Religion

Consider so-called morality plays: fictional works conveying moral and prudential lessons. One common type of morality play is 'tragedy' or 'tragic drama'. A central lesson of tragedies is this: although violating (plausible[41]) moral norms may appear to the acting agent to have greater expected personal benefits than moral behavior, it is nevertheless imprudent to risk violating such norms, given how immoral actions can lead to maximally regrettable outcomes that moral actions typically do not have.

Consider the standard plot of tragedies. Typically, the protagonist risks violating moral norms because it appears to them to have the best-expected outcome. However, their risk goes horribly wrong. Unexpected events cause their moral transgressions to result in prudential disaster—disaster that they regret far more than they likely would have regretted had they obeyed moral norms. The lesson implicit in tragedies, as such, is that prudent people should not risk violating moral norms because of just how much they might regret it. Let us call this first trope of morality plays *immorality is not worth the risk of maximal regret*.

This trope is widely embedded in tragedies across history and cultures. *Hamlet* is considered as one of the most powerful tragedies in world literature. Why is *Hamlet* so tragic? Upon close examination, we see that not just one but three main characters suffer maximally regrettable personal misfortune for risking immoral behavior. At the outset, we are introduced to King Hamlet, the recently deceased king of Denmark, who we learn slew King Fortinbras of Norway many years ago (a 'moral risk' insofar as killing people is generally immoral). Shortly thereafter, Prince Hamlet encounters his father's ghost, who tells him that his brother Claudius (Prince Hamlet's uncle) murdered him to seize the throne and marry his widow, Queen Gertrude. After encouraging Prince Hamlet to seek revenge on Claudius (another 'moral risk' by King Hamlet, since 'taking the law into your own hands' is plausibly immoral), Prince Hamlet hatches a plan to kill Claudius and avenge his father's death (Prince Hamlet's first 'moral risk'). Alas, the plan goes horribly wrong. When Hamlet goes to kill Claudius, he finds Claudius praying and—because Hamlet reasons that Claudius would go to heaven if killed while praying—Hamlet relents. This causes Claudius to fear Hamlet, leading Claudius to hatch a plan to kill Hamlet in return (Claudius' 'moral risk'). Finally, after Hamlet tragically kills another innocent character (Polonius) as a result of mistaken identity (another 'moral risk' on Hamlet's part), Hamlet and Claudius end up killing each other, Queen Gertrude is killed, Hamlet's entire royal family is murdered, and the new King Fortinbras—the son of the former king killed by the original King Hamlet—seizes the Danish throne.

Hamlet is such a powerful story—a moral and prudential tragedy *par excellence*—because each character's willingness to risk violating moral norms unexpectedly leads to profoundly regrettable outcomes for them and others they care about. King Hamlet's 'moral risks' (invading Norway, killing another king, and encouraging his son to seek revenge) unexpectedly lead to the loss of everything he valued during his lifetime: his kingdom and family. Similarly, Prince Hamlet's 'moral risks' (plotting to kill Claudius and killing

Polonius by mistake) unexpectedly result in him losing everything he values: his life, the throne, and his family's lives. Finally, Claudius' 'moral risk' (plotting to kill Hamlet) results in *him* losing his life and the throne. The moral and prudential lesson of Hamlet thus seems to be this:

> Do not be like King Hamlet, Prince Hamlet, or Claudius. Although violating moral norms may appear to have the best-expected outcomes, it is not worth the risk. Life is profoundly uncertain and the potential disasters that immoral actions can cause are maximally regrettable, far more regrettable that doing the morally safe thing.

Hamlet is far from alone in presenting this lesson. It is a common storytelling trope across history and cultures. Many modern works of tragic-fiction illustrate the same lesson.[42] We also see it in ancient works, such as Old Testament stories ranging from Adam and Eve's expulsion from the Garden of Eden for disobeying God's commands (which Christians consider to be moral requirements), to God punishing King David for infidelity and the treachery of sending Bathsheba's husband off to be killed in battle. We also see the trope in non-Western heroic fiction. For example, in a recent 'Bollywood' film,[43] a corrupt police officer cooperates with two drug dealers, accepting bribes in return for letting them continue their illegal activities. Later, through chance events, the drug dealers brutally rape a young woman the police officer unexpectedly falls in love with. This devastates the corrupt officer, leading him to regret his past corruption, change his ways, and become a hero. Similarly, in Asian martial arts films, the following is a common type of plot: a powerful mob boss immorally kills the protagonist's family or loved-ones. Then, months or years later, the protagonist uses their martial-arts mastery to avenge their deaths, killing the boss's henchmen, and ultimately, the boss themselves.[44] In every case, the implicit moral-prudential lesson seems to be this: 'Do not be like Adam and Eve, King David, the corrupt police officer, evil henchmen, or the mob boss. Do not risk violating moral norms because it seems to have likely positive benefits: you might profoundly regret it'.

Now, in tragedies, the tragic characters are typically never able to learn from their moral-prudential mistake(s) until it is too late—that is, until after their death or death of their loved ones. This is what makes such stories so powerful. However, another genre of

Outline of a Theory of Prudence 35

morality play just mentioned—heroic fiction—typically combines this first moral-prudential lesson with another: the trope that *morality has better likely personal outcomes in the long-term*. Indeed, both tropes together constitute a distinct subtype of morality play: *redemption stories*. In redemption stories, the protagonist typically begins as a 'rogue'—a thief, smuggler, or criminal who risks violating moral norms in pursuit of personal gain.[45] However, after their actions unexpectedly result in prudentially disastrous outcomes they regret, they get a 'second chance.' Instead of their story ending in tragedy, the hero learns their lesson: they become no longer willing to risk violating moral norms, and instead come to treat the expected long-term aggregate benefit of moral behavior as greater than the expected benefits of immoral behavior.

For example, in a recent popular film, a young warrior prince disobeys his father, the King, thus destroying a fragile truce between two factions—a 'moral risk' in the sense that the prince's presumptive obligation is to serve the King.[46] The King then banishes the prince from the kingdom, punishing the prince for his transgression. For a time, the prince is dejected and hopeless, regretting his transgression. His regrets, however, lead him to change his ways, culminating in him choosing moral behavior even when it appears imprudent: he chooses to sacrifice himself to save the lives of his friends. Fortunately, to the hero's surprise, the events that led him to sacrifice himself turn out to be a test his father created to see whether he learned his lesson. In the end, the prince is welcomed back into the kingdom as a hero. The implicit lesson here, and in many redemption-stories like it, is:

> Learn the moral-prudential lesson the prince learned. Even when moral behavior does not seem like it will benefit you, if you are patient and stick to it, then it probably will benefit you in the long run, far more than immoral behavior is likely to.

Morality plays thus tend to contain two related moral-prudential lessons: a negative lesson and a positive one. The negative lesson of tragedies is that, given life's great uncertainty, violating moral norms is not worth the risk because of the immensely regrettable outcomes immoral actions can cause. The negative lesson, in short, appears to be that life's uncertainties should lead one to (A) act on minimax regret, and by extension (B) avoid immoral behavior, because (C) one can regret immoral behavior far more than moral behavior. The positive lesson of redemption-stories then is that one should internalize the negative attitudes just described—avoiding immoral behavior on minimax regret grounds—precisely because this strategy ('moral risk-aversion') has greater expected aggregate personal lifetime benefits than immorality.

These same lessons are also implicitly embedded in doctrines of divine or cosmic justice across a wide variety of world religions. Many religions envision heaven as a long-term reward for moral behavior and hell as punishment for evil. Similarly, in Hinduism, moral behavior is seen as rewarded and bad behavior punished in reincarnation via *karma*. Taken literally, these doctrines teach that it is certain that one will be eternally rewarded for good and punished for evil. However, given our epistemic situation—that is, given that the existence of heaven, hell, reincarnation, and so on, can seem remote and uncertain—these doctrines implicitly convey the same two moral-prudential lessons as tragedies and redemption-stories. The doctrine of hell conveys that immorality is not worth the maximally regrettable risk of divine punishment. Conversely, the doctrine of heaven conveys that morality is likely to result in greater long-term benefits. These are the same moral-prudential lessons as in morality plays: they aim to convince the hearer that immorality is not worth the risk of greater maximal regret, and that morality has greater expected long-term value.

Notice, finally, how closely these lessons hew to Bruckner's theory of prudence. Bruckner holds that prudence requires minimax regret given life's uncertainty, and that the more we care about the past and future, the more this rule should converge with maximization of expected long-term personal benefit. This is what morality plays teach, with the added substantive claims that (A) given certain empirical regularities (viz. observed consequences of moral and immoral behavior), (B) prudent agents *should* care a great deal about the past and future, (C) learning from the maximally regrettable consequences of moral mistakes (by ourselves and others), such that (D) we should treat immoral behavior as not worth the risk (viz. minimax regret), and instead (E) internalize attitudes that moral behavior has greater expected long-term aggregate value.

Finally, morality plays also convey a further lesson that will prove to be important in Chapter 3: specifically, that how one sees the likelihoods—of whether moral or immoral action is likely to have better personal outcomes—depends on whether one has internalized the above moral-prudential lessons in one's own attitudes (i.e. one's beliefs and desires). Prior to 'learning their lesson'—that is, prior to internalizing 'moral risk-aversion'—characters in redemption-stories perceive the likely benefits of immoral behavior as outweighing the risk. However, after learning their lesson, they see things the opposite way, judging the benefits of immorality to be a mirage, believing instead that the long-term benefits of moral behavior are greater.

The next question is whether these moral-prudential lessons are actually true for real human agents, morality plays and religious myths aside. We will now see that there are ample reasons to think that prudent people do indeed tend to internalize the above lessons in their standing psychological attitudes, precisely because of life's great uncertainty. Chapter 3 will then outline how a normative moral and social-political theory, Rightness as Fairness, is derivable from this prudential foundation. Chapter 4 will then detail how this unified theory of prudence and morality explains a variety of philosophical and empirical phenomena. Finally, Chapter 5 will consider potential counterexamples.

4.2 The Prudence of Learned 'Moral Risk-Aversion' in Childhood

Consider childhood and adolescent television programming: so-called after-school specials that present moral and prudential lessons to children. A typical storyline here involves a child or adolescent choosing to risk violating moral norms for some expected benefit, such as lying to their parents to attend a music concert. The child usually hatches a 'perfect plan' for getting away with the risk. Alas, as in tragic dramas, unexpected events lead the child to suffer negative consequences they highly regret, such as punishment by parents, school officials, or law enforcement. Finally, however, like redemption-stories, such programs usually end on a happy note, with the child or adolescent coming to believe that violating moral norms is not worth the risk, and that moral behavior has better long-term benefits than immorality.

We can see how ubiquitous these moral-prudential lessons are by considering a few examples. In one television episode in a series targeting children,[47] a father allows his daughter to use his credit-card as a reward for academic success.[48] The daughter then succumbs to temptation, going overboard with her spending, in turn hatching several different plans with her classmates—all of which violate moral norms—to earn back the money. However, every plan backfires, leading her to eventually regret her behavior and 'come clean' to her father, who then rewards her for telling the truth. Similarly, in a more fanciful episode, a teenager is struck by lightning, enabling him to see the future.[49] The character then uses this power to help a friend cheat on an exam. The power wears off, however, and his friend fails the exam due to lack of preparation—leading them both to regret their plan. Finally, in a third episode, a teenager goes to dangerous lengths to get a female student to go to a school dance, bugging the girl's bedroom with microphones to overhear her conversations with female friends.[50] Unfortunately for the boy, the young women find out and take revenge on him, leading him to regret his actions.

As we see in these stories and many others, the same two moral-prudential lessons depicted in tragic fiction and redemption-stories are common in youth television programming. Such programs give children many examples, in vivid contexts they understand, of how violating moral norms is not worth the risk of immense regret, and how moral behavior has greater expected long-term benefits.

These lessons are also typically socially reinforced in children on an everyday basis. In early childhood, young children often misbehave, risking violating moral norms as a result of impulsivity, such as playing in the house when their parents tell them not to, getting into fights on the playground, or engaging in minor forms of theft. Here, though, is what often happens. Although the child commits these acts impulsively, children who are well-supervised and well-raised are regularly caught and punished for such behavior. Typically (though not always), such forms of punishment lead to regret—if only for 'getting caught'. Finally, children are also socialized to believe there are greater longer-term benefits—such as good performance at school, as well as parental and other social rewards—if they *do* obey moral norms. Consequently, unless they have psychopathic tendencies,[51] the typical child will learn to internalize the above empirical regularities in their attitudes. They will come to believe, on the basis of empirical regularities they observe around them, that (A) immoral behavior is not worth the risk of immense regret, and (B) moral behavior has greater expected long-term personal benefits, in turn developing (C) standing negative desires not to behave immorally, and (D) standing positive desires to act morally as a general 'life policy'.

In other words, childhood moral-prudential learning appears to occur in three stages (Figure 2.1). In Stage 1, children risk violating moral norms but are (at least occasionally) punished or see other children punished for similar behavior. This tends to lead them to learn, in Stage 2, that it is imprudent to risk violating moral norms

Stage 1: socially-punished moral-norm violations

Impulsivity/present focus	Violation of moral norm	External Punishment	Regret
Temptation to steal candy. Desire to hit another child. Cheating on school test.	→ *First-personal*: Stealing candy. *Second/third-personal*: observing schoolyard fight or cheating.	→ Parental discipline. School suspension. Legal punishment.	→ 'I wish I hadn't stolen the candy.' 'It was stupid for Jones to get in a fight. They got in trouble.'

Stage 2: externally-incentivized 'moral risk-aversion'

Temptation/present focus	Memory of punishment & regret	Minimax regret / moral-risk aversion	Delayed social reward
Temptation to steal candy. Desire to hit another child. Cheating on school test.	→ *First-personal*: 'I don't want to get in trouble for that again'. *Second/third-personal*: 'Jones got suspended from school for that'.	→ 'I shouldn't risk stealing, fighting, or cheating. I might regret it. It's not worth the risk'.	→ Parent rewards good behavior. Better friendships at school. Good academic performance.

Stage 3: internalized 'moral risk-aversion'

Internalized moral-risk aversion	Temptation to immorality	Internalized moral-risk aversion	Delayed internal reward
'I shouldn't get into fights, steal candy, or cheat on tests. I might regret it. And I see that people tend to benefit more later when they follow the rules'.	→ Impulse to steal candy or hit another child. Etc.	→ 'I don't want to risk it. If I do, I might feel guilty and regret it'.	→ 'I'm proud of myself, and my parents and teachers would be proud that I followed the rules'.

Figure 2.1 Childhood Moral-Prudential Learning.

because their parents or other authority figures may punish them and instead reward moral behavior in the longer run. Finally, in Stage 3, the child internalizes this reward-punishment structure into their own beliefs and preferences by believing they should behave morally, wanting to behave morally, punishing themselves (viz. guilt) if they are tempted to violate moral norms (and even more severely if they do violate moral norms), and rewarding themselves (viz. inner self-esteem) if they 'do the right thing'.

4.3 The Prudence of Consolidating 'Moral Risk-Aversion' in Adolescence

This schema is not only typically repeated throughout childhood. It ordinarily continues well into adolescence and adulthood. Sometimes adolescents simply extend the moral-prudential lessons they learned as children to new situations—for instance, avoiding cheating on exams in high school and beyond because of the standing negative attitudes (against risking violating moral norms) and positive attitudes (in favor of obeying moral norms) they began internalizing as children. Other times, however, adolescents can fail to generalize the moral-prudential lessons from childhood to new cases. Consider the kinds of risky violations of moral norms that adolescents may engage in: cheating on school exams, cutting class to do drugs with friends, sneaking out of the home to go to a party or concert, and so on. Here again, as in childhood, the same pattern of moral-prudential learning typically appears to play out (Figure 2.2). The adolescent who fails to study for an exam may be tempted to cheat, figuring they are likely to succeed. Perhaps they even cheat successfully a few times. However, what often happens is that they are eventually—and, from their standpoint, unexpectedly—caught. The end-result is punishment, which can range in severity: they may end up failing the exam, get sent to the principal's office, receive detention or a school suspension, or face parental punishment at home (Stage 4). In more severe cases, such as drug use or petty crime, adolescents may be subject to serious legal ramifications. These are negative outcomes which, if the adolescent is not a criminal delinquent or a psychopath, they will typically find highly regrettable: far more regrettable than outcomes they experience when they behave morally (where, e.g. the worst they can do is perform poorly on an exam). Next, just as in childhood, these lessons are often also reinforced by second and third-hand experience: by the adolescent seeing what happens to others around them

Stage 4: negative consequences of failures to extend 'moral risk-aversion' to adolescent choices

<u>Temptation to immorality</u> 'I learned as a child that I shouldn't get in fights on the schoolyard or steal candy. But I think I can cheat on my high-school exam and sneak out to a concert, get away with it, and not feel guilty'.	<u>Immoral behavior (first-personal)</u> Cheating on exam. Sneaking out of house. ↑ <u>Observed immorality (third-personal)</u> Hearing friend cheated on exam. Hearing friend snuck out of home.	<u>External and/or Internal Punishment</u> Parental, school, legal punishment 'I got away with it, but I feel guilty for cheating and lying to everyone'. → <u>Observed External / Internal Punishment</u> Others face parental, school, legal sanctions. Seeing friends feel guilty for their actions.	<u>Consolidation of 'moral risk-aversion'</u> 'It is so dumb to cheat on exams, sneak out of the house, or do drugs. I've either gotten punished myself, felt guilty for it, or seen others get punished or feel guilty. Violating social moral norms is not worth the risk: I might regret it far worse than behaving morally, and I have seen the lives of people my age go better on the whole when they behave morally. They have better friends, go to college, and so on'.

Stage 5: consolidated 'moral risk-aversion' (conscience)

<u>Consolidated 'moral risk-aversion'</u> 'I don't want to cheat, sneak out, or use drugs. I know that it's a bad risk I might regret, both because of potential social punishment but also because I have learned to feel guilty for bad behavior'.	<u>Temptation to immorality</u> 'Blanking out' at an exam, and being tempted to look at another student's exam.	<u>Prospective guilt/regret</u> 'I shouldn't risk cheating. I might regret it. I might end up expelled, unable to go to college, or just feel guilty and have to confess to get the guilt off my chest'.	<u>Delayed internal and/or external rewards</u> 'I might not get the best grade on the exam. But I am proud that I didn't cheat. I might have regretted it far worse than a bad grade. I can always study harder and do better next time'.

Figure 2.2 Adolescent Moral-Prudential Consolidation.

who violate moral norms (other adolescents being expelled from school, arrested by police, and so on)—presenting them, just as in childhood, with the following empirical regularities: adolescents like them tending to regret choices to risk violating moral norms, and benefitting more over the long-term by behaving morally.

Consequently, the prudent adolescent (at least typically) comes to progressively believe that violating moral norms is not worth the risk of immense regret (viz. minimax regret), and that moral behavior has better expected aggregate value over the long run given life's many uncertainties (Stage 5). Further, if they are prudent, they consolidate these beliefs into standing desires: negative desires not to risk violating moral norms *in general*, and positive desires to obey moral norms for longer-term benefit. These attitudes in turn constitute and give rise to a progressive number of other attitudes and dispositions readily identifiable (in commonsense) as 'having a conscience': the adolescent increasingly believes they shouldn't violate moral norms, desires not to violate them, worries about what might happen if they do violate them, feels guilt and regret when they do, and so on.

4.4 The Prudence of Consolidating Categorical 'Moral Risk-Aversion' in Adulthood

Finally, the same learning process often continues to play itself out—with increasingly high stakes—in adulthood. Once in adulthood, people either make moral and prudential mistakes of their own (often with very serious consequences) or observe others doing so. For example, some people fall prey to the temptation to drive under the influence of drugs or alcohol—often suffering extreme consequences, such as a serious car crash or jail time. Alternatively, they may witness dire consequences for others who engage in these behaviors—for instance, friends or associates dying in a vehicular accident or suffering jail time for driving under the influence. Similarly, some adults succumb to temptation of infidelity, cheating on a romantic partner or spouse. Although romantic or sexual affairs can be tempting, one common result is that the affair is found out and the person's primary romantic relationship irreparably damaged, something that can lead to great, long-lasting regret ('I wish I had never cheated. I ruined everything with someone I love'.). Further, even if an adult does not make these mistakes themselves, chances are they will often see others suffer long-term from such decisions.

For example, consider recent sexual misconduct scandals. Although many alleged perpetrators got away with such behavior for years or even decades, many are now facing serious consequences.[52] Second, consider pseudonymous philosophy blogs.[53] Many such forums flourished for a time, hosting content alleged by some to involve unethical forms of abuse or defamation.[54] However, each forum eventually closed down because the blog administrators were either unexpectedly found out or found themselves in danger of having their identity revealed.[55] These cases both fit with the theory of prudence proposed above. For although sexual harassers and owners of pseudonymous blogs might have thought they could benefit from their actions, the seemingly unlikely happened: their actions and identities were either revealed or threatened to be revealed, putting their future in jeopardy in ways they could (and perhaps did) end up deeply regretting.

What prudent adults typically do, then, is observe these kinds of empirical regularities—the same kinds of empirical regularities they observed in childhood and adolescence—but now with even greater stakes. We often see just how profoundly, and in many cases unexpectedly, immoral behavior can negatively impact perpetrators' lives, ruining their careers, marriages, public reputation, well-being, and autonomy—up to and including legal ramifications or even death. Conversely, we also normally see how moral behavior appears beneficial in the long-term, enabling people to cultivate stable careers, families, and long-term well-being by 'doing things the right way'. Consequently, assuming they have already internalized morally risk-averse attitudes in childhood and adolescence—becoming prudent people 'of conscience'—prudent adults typically consolidate these morally risk-averse attitudes in the strongest way possible, internalizing them as a set of *categorical* attitudes (Figure 2.3): (i) negative attitudes (beliefs and desires) that immoral behaviors are never worth the risk of immense regret, and (ii) positive attitudes that they should always behave morally regardless of what else they might desire. This is the final stage of moral-prudential learning (Stage 7).

In sum, throughout childhood, adolescence, and adulthood, the very same prudential lessons that we observe in fictional tragedies, redemption-stories, and world religions appear to be both externally incentivized by empirical social regularities, and then—at least typically—progressively internalized by prudent individuals in their own attitudes. This process culminates in the internalization of 'categorical' attitudes that violating moral norms is never

Stage 6: negative consequences for failures to categorically extend 'moral risk-aversion' to adult choices

Temptation to immorality
Getting into a car intoxicated. Opportunity for infidelity. Desire to engage in salacious anonymous online gossip. Etc.

→ **Immoral behavior**
Driving drunk, engaging in infidelity, online gossip, etc.

→ **External and/or internal punishment**
DUI conviction, failed relationship or marriage, unexpected negative professional consequences, internal worry, regret, and guilt, etc.

Witnessing immoral behavior
Knowing/hearing of others driving drunk, engaging in infidelity, online gossip, etc.

→ **Observed external & internal punishment**
Seeing others suffer the above types of consequences.

→ **Categorical internalization of 'moral risk-aversion'**
'It is always (categorically) imprudent to drive drunk, engage in infidelity, or otherwise violate moral norms, even if it looks like I might benefit. For I have learned in my own case and by observing others' lives that immoral behavior is not worth the risk. One can regret immoral behavior more than anything, and one's life is likely to go better in the long run if you always (categorically) do what is morally right'.

Stage 7: internalization of categorically 'morally risk-averse' attitudes

Categorical 'moral risk-aversion'
'I shouldn't ever risk violating moral norms. I have learned I might regret it far more than obeying them'.

Categorical moral commitment
'I want to be a good person who does what's right "for its own sake". Even when it might not appear to benefit me, there's dignity in doing the right thing'.

→ **Temptation to immorality**
Tempting opportunity to engage in infidelity, illegal behavior, or behavior that otherwise violates moral norms.

→ **Desire to act in moral ways one *knows* one will not regret**
'I have been punished or felt guilty in the past (in childhood, adolescence, and adulthood) when I've risked violating moral norms. I want to act in a way I *know* I will not regret, and I believe that I will not regret (categorically) committing myself to behaving morally for its own sake'.

→ **Delayed internal and/or external reward**
'I wish I wasn't tempted to begin with, but I feel good that I had the strength to do the right thing. I also know that doing the right thing tends to have better long-term outcomes. People recognize my honesty, and being a good person has resulted in many long-term goods: a good career, marriage, friendships and so on, things that I have seen other people regret destroying through bad behavior'.

Figure 2.3 Adult Categorical Moral-Prudential Consolidation.

worth the risk of immense regret (viz. minimax regret), and morality always has better expected long-term value (viz. lifetime aggregate utility maximization), given life's immense uncertainties. Importantly, this account coheres with well-established facts of moral development: namely, that children first obey moral norms on largely instrumental grounds,[56] but over time progressively internalize a commitment to act on moral principles for their own sake[57]—though even then, elements of instrumental reasoning still remain prominent.[58]

5 Outline of a Normative Theory of Prudence

This chapter's theory of prudence is as follows (Figure 2.4). First, diachronic instrumental rationality is prudence's highest-level normative requirement: prudence is a matter of acting in ways that have the best-expected aggregate outcomes for an agent's life as a whole. Second, because life as a whole is radically uncertain, a prudent agent should treat an action as rational only if it conforms to principles of prudence that are instrumentally rational from a standpoint of radical uncertainty: a Prudential Original Position. Third, the principle of prudence most rational from that standpoint appears to be minimax regret. Fourth, due to observed empirical regularities, minimax regret in real life typically leads prudent agents to become deeply averse to risking violating moral norms (viz. 'moral risk-aversion'), and—because morally risk-averse individuals learn to care a great deal about the past and future—to regard this strategy as maximizing expected aggregate utility over the course of their life as a whole (viz. moral behavior). Consequently, what appears to be a form of prudential risk-aversion (unwillingness to risk immoral behavior) just is a form of long-term self-control (delaying immediate gratification viz. temptation to immorality, for the sake of greater long-term expected benefits of moral behavior). Thus, descending from the highest-level requirement of prudence—that prudence involves maximizing aggregate expected utility over life as a whole—prudence at a first-order level is (at least typically) a matter of 'morally-constrained aggregate-lifetime-utility maximization'. An action is prudent for an agent if and only if it has the best-expected aggregate lifetime personal utility (viz. rationally weighing and aggregating costs and benefits[59]) constrained by standing negative categorical attitudes (beliefs and desires) against ever violating moral norms and positive categorical attitudes in favor of 'behaving morally for its own sake'.

Highest-level normative requirement

- **Diachronic instrumental rationality:** An action is prudent for an agent if and only if it has the best-expected aggregate lifetime value.

- **Rational choice under radical diachronic uncertainty:** Because life as a whole is deeply uncertain, an action has the best-expected aggregate lifetime value for an agent only if it conforms to *principles of prudence* that are rational on an assumption of radical uncertainty.

- **Rational choice from a Prudential Original Position:** Because a Prudential Original Position represents choice under radical uncertainty, an action is prudent for an agent only if it is consistent with whichever principle(s) are instrumentally rational from a Prudential Original Position.

- **Minimax regret:** The most instrumentally rational principle from a Prudential Original Position is minimax regret.

- **Categorical 'moral risk-aversion':** Prudent individuals typically learn on the basis of empirical regularities to treat the maximum possible regret resulting from immoral behavior as always greater than for moral behavior. Thus, an action is (typically) prudent for an agent only if it is consistent with or based on standing, internalized attitudes to categorically avoid risking violating moral norms.

- **Categorical moral commitment:** Prudent individuals also typically learn on the basis of empirical regularities that, given life's uncertainty, 'categorically' committing to acting on moral norms 'for their own sake' has greater expected aggregate lifetime value than alternatives, even in cases where immoral behavior may appear to have better expected outcomes. Thus, an action is (typically) prudent for an agent only if it is consistent with or based upon standing, internalized attitudes to categorically obey moral norms 'for their own sake.'

First-level normative requirement

- **Morally-constrained utility-maximization:** An action is (typically) prudent for an agent if and only if it (A) has the best-expected aggregate lifetime value given (B) standing negative attitudes of categorical 'moral risk-aversion', and (C) standing positive attitudes to categorically obey moral norms 'for their own sake'.

Figure 2.4 Outline of a Normative Theory of Prudence.

Outline of a Theory of Prudence 47

This book does not aim to prove this theory. As Chapter 5 examines, there may be plausible counterexamples (which, hopefully, are outliers). The point for now is simply that there is much to be said for this account when considering moral-prudential development, the empirical regularities that underlie it, and the ubiquity of moral-prudential lessons in tragic fiction, redemption-stories, and other cultural artifacts across cultures and different eras.

Now, a theory may be reflected in common social practices and yet still be false. So let us look a bit deeper. Why do prudent people appear to focus so much on minimizing maximum possible regret, at least when it comes to avoiding violating moral norms? Second, why do we tend to think that immorality is liable to generate greater possible regrets than moral behavior? Isn't it possible to regret moral behavior just as immensely as immoral behavior? Third, why do we tend to think morality is more beneficial over the long-term than immorality? I believe there is a more general social-psychological story we can tell here to buttress the normative plausibility of this chapter's theory in response to these kinds of questions.

First, typical human adults display a pronounced negativity bias, such that when it comes to outcomes of equal positive and negative intensity, negative outcomes weigh far more heavily in determining our thoughts and actions.[60] Human beings also display proclivities to loss-aversion, with some studies indicating that perceived losses are twice as powerful, psychologically, as prospective gains.[61] In concrete terms, people tend to disprefer a loss of $100 about twice as much as they prefer a gain of $100. People also tend to display status quo bias, preferring things to remain as they are rather than change,[62] as well as dispositions to keep things they already have (the endowment effect).[63] Finally, as noted in Chapter 1, risk-aversion is known to be implicated in prudential cognition.[64] People tend to weigh improbable events more heavily than moderate or high-probability ones, be highly averse to even a small chance of severe loss, and desire 'sure things' over moderate or even high-probability gains.[65] People also appear to derive more utility from guaranteed good outcomes than they do from risky good outcomes of equal expected value.[66]

Are there any good normative grounds for these psychological phenomena? One plausible answer is that they are rational responses to immense lifetime uncertainty: if one does not know how the future is likely to go, then keeping what you already have is a sure thing—it protects your future from unexpected jeopardy.

The problem with immoral actions, or so we learn from experience, is that although they can produce immense gains (e.g. riches, power), they are risks that can produce immense losses, both externally *and* internally. Consider social ostracism (e.g. job and reputation loss) for violating moral norms or going to jail for violating moral and legal norms. Both can systematically undermine a person's ability to pursue their goals for many years to come. Further, for a person who has internalized minimax regret (given human dispositions to negativity bias, etc.), the internal worry or guilt they may experience from violating moral norms may be long-lasting. For example, an individual who cheats on their spouse may not only end up divorced and alone, but also regretting their actions 'for the rest of their life'. Conversely, moral actions rarely appear to have these kinds of intensely negative consequences. First, the maximum negative consequences of moral behavior tend to be not losses from the status quo, but rather foregone gains: wealth or power with which one may have no prior experience. Second, for a person who has internalized the desire to behave morally based on the belief that morality has greater additive value over their life, even when things go poorly externally (e.g. one could have become rich by stealing), one can at least take solace in having done the 'right thing'. Moral actions, in other words, tend to be *regarded* by prudent people as far less potentially regrettable than immoral actions. And to the person who has internalized this kind of moral risk-aversion—the person who wants to behave morally because they believe it has better long-term outcomes and is less-regrettable—moral actions contain very little risk, and the prospect of at least some sure reward: a sense of internal pride for having 'done the right thing'.

Consequently, this chapter's theory of prudence appears to have good normative foundations. 'Moral risk-aversion'—aversion to risking violating moral norms, and instead categorically preferring to behave morally for its own sake—appears to be an effective long-term means to preserving one's social and economic status, personal autonomy, and internal well-being. Conversely, willingness to risk immoral behavior places all of these features of our lives in serious jeopardy, as illustrated by examples of criminals, psychopaths, and ordinary people (including, often enough, ourselves) who routinely suffer serious long-term consequences for immoral behavior.

None of this is to say that everyone internalizes 'moral risk-aversion', or that it is always prudent. Some people become criminals; others become habitual 'cheaters' in romantic relationships; and so on—and some people appear to fare well in life through immoral means. It remains an open question whether such behaviors can be prudent. We will return to these potential counterexamples in Chapter 5.

6 Outline of Descriptive Psychological Theory of Prudence

Finally, let us reflect on the psychology of a person who has internalized this chapter's account of prudential 'moral risk-aversion'. How will such a person approach first-order life-decisions? Consider first negative categorical attitudes against ever risking violating moral norms on minimax regret grounds. A person who has internalized these standing attitudes will approach morally salient cases by wanting to avoid even the smallest likelihood of acting in an immoral way they might deeply regret. Second, if they have developed the standing positive categorical attitudes that I have argued are (typically) prudent, they will have positive attitudes of the following sort: 'Whatever happens, if I do the right thing for its own sake, I will *regret it less* than if I do the wrong thing'. In sum, Figure 2.5 represents the psychology of a person who conforms to this chapter's theory of prudence.

Is this the moral-prudential psychology that prudent people exhibit in everyday life? It indeed appears to be. For consider again an opportunity to cheat on an exam or a romantic partner. Everyone knows it is possible to get away with these kinds of actions. In some cases, it may even seem likely. However, prudent people typically become unwilling to take these risks. Why? *We worry we might regret it.* We also tend to believe that moral behavior is advantageous in the long-run (viz. sayings like 'honesty is the best policy'). We also tend to *want* to behave morally ('I want to do the right thing'), wanting to know 'the right thing to do' before making a choice so that we can derive inner-satisfaction from doing the right thing 'for its own sake'. Finally, we even tend to counsel others in these terms when they struggle with temptation, impressing the rationality of moral risk-aversion upon them in minimax regret terms (e.g. 'Don't do go through with cheating on your partner. You might regret it more than anything!'), the long-term benefits of moral behavior ('Cheaters never prosper'), and morality's internal benefits ('If you tell the truth, you will at least have a clear conscience'), and so on.

RETROSPECTIVE CONCERNS (PAST)

Memory of potential regrets for immoral behavior (first-, second-, and third-personal)
- Social punishment
- Internal punishment (guilt)
- Fictional moral tragedies
- Hell narratives for immoral behavior
- Etc.

RETROSPECTIVE CONCERNS (PAST)

Memory of delayed rewards for moral behavior (first-, second-, and third-personal)
- External rewards (from parents, etc.)
- Internal rewards (self-esteem)
- Redemption stories
- Heaven narratives for good behavior
- Etc.

PRUDENT AGENT (PRESENT)

Internalized Attitudes

1. Aim to act in ways w/best-expected lifetime outcomes.
2. Standing (implicit) commitment to minimax regret.
3. Standing beliefs that, given life's uncertainty and observed empirical regularities that:
   A. Immorality has greater possible regret than morality.
   B. Morality has greater long-term benefits.
4. From 1-3, internalization of:
   i. Categorical moral risk-aversion
   ii. Categorical commitment to moral behavior
5. **Morally-constrained utility-maximization**: aim to maximize expected lifetime value constrained by categorical moral-risk aversion and moral commitment.

PROSPECTIVE CONCERNS (FUTURE)

Temptation to immorality
'I am so tempted to lie. I think I probably would not get caught, and it looks like I might benefit'.

'Moral Risk-Aversion' (MRA) - viz. Minimax Regret
'I do not want to risk doing something I might deeply regret. I want to make a choice I know I will not regret'.

Categorical Negative MRA	Categorical Positive MRA
'I don't want to risk telling the lie. I might regret it'.	'I should tell the truth for its own sake. I won't regret it'.

Morally-constrained utility-maximization
'I will aim to make whichever choices are best for my life, but only within moral bounds'.

Figure 2.5 A Descriptive Model of Prudential Psychology.

7 Three Clarifications

Three points are worth clarifying. First, this theory does not hold that prudent agents should directly use minimax regret to make first-order life decisions, such as what to eat or which career to choose. As we have seen, Bruckner argues that prudence requires minimax regret as a high-level principle, but that the more an agent cares about the past or future, the more an agent following minimax regret will *appear* to be acting on a simple principle of expected-personal-utility maximization.[67] This chapter's theory coheres with this result: it holds that normatively prudent agents typically internalize morally risk-averse attitudes on minimax regret grounds, but that these attitudes should lead prudent individuals to act as though they are engaging in 'morally-constrained utility-maximization', making everyday choices that appear to them to *maximize their own long-term well-being* within moral constraints. I believe this result accurately represents how prudent people typically make decisions. Prudent people like you and I typically seek to make choices that maximize our own long-term benefit constrained by our 'moral conscience'.

Second, the theory does not hold that most people actually tend to care about their past or future when making decisions. As we have seen, empirical science has found that people are often present-focused, treating their past and future selves akin to strangers.[68] The theory defended here merely holds that *normatively prudent* people care about their past and future in the broad sense of aiming to live happy lives as a whole, as well as in specifically morally salient cases, recalling and regretting past punishment for immoral behavior, and not wanting to risk potential future regret when temptations to immorality arise. I argued this is also intuitive, as prudent people appear to respond to moral temptations this way: namely, by recalling past regrets and worrying about potential future regret. Further, empirical science suggests these are indeed central features distinguishing prudent, moral people from criminals and psychopaths. Psychopaths lack retrospective regret for their past immoral behavior,[69] and criminals and psychopaths appear to engage in imprudent and immoral behavior because of not worrying about the future[70] or being able to use experiences of prospective regret to inhibit immoral behavior.[71]

Finally—and this is important—this chapter has not argued that 'moral risk-aversion' always has greater expected aggregate lifetime personal utility than immoral behavior. As Chapter 5 discusses, there may be cases where immoral actions have better-expected long-term outcomes than moral behavior. My argument in this chapter has merely been that across childhood, adolescence, and adulthood, prudent individuals typically learn to internalize attitudes that *treat* moral actions as always having greater expected lifetime personal outcomes than immoral ones. I argued that this is because prudent individuals appreciate how life as a whole is profoundly uncertain, while internalizing two broad empirical regularities: (1) people often paying dearly for and regretting immoral behavior, and (2) moral behavior tending to pay off in the long-run (viz. stable and productive lives, careers, relationships, and so on). Consequently, my theory has not been that moral actions always in fact have greater expected lifetime value than immoral ones. Rather, it is that prudent agents typically internalize attitudes that *treat* moral actions as having greater expected lifetime value—as a kind of 'safe' life policy for grappling with the otherwise-uncertain nature of life as a whole. We have seen that this is amply attested to in moral-prudential development, as well as in common adages such as 'Honesty is the best policy'. Although most of us recognize (at least implicitly) that it may be possible for immoral actions like dishonesty to pay off, prudent people typically appear to internalize the opposite attitude: that moral actions such as honesty are better 'life-policies' likely to have better aggregate long term outcomes than immoral behavior.

8 Conclusion

Chapter 3 will now argue that this theory of prudence and prudential cognition entails a novel normative theory of morality and empirical theory of moral cognition. Chapter 4 will then argue that this unified theory of prudence and morality is the best normative and descriptive explanation currently available of the behavioral neuroscience summarized in Chapter 1.

Notes

1 Kant [1785, 1788, 1797]. Cf. Baron (2005), Korsgaard (1996), Wood (2008).
2 Lord (2018), Parfit (2001, 2011), Scanlon (2014). Cf. Broome (2007), Lang (2012), Smith (2017).
3 Paul (2015a, 2015b), Arvan (2016): ch 1, §3.
4 Anand (1995), Hansson (2005), Peterson (2017), Steele and Stefánsson (2016).

5 Aristotle [1984]. *Nicomachean Ethics*: Book VI, esp. 1140a, 1141b, 1142b.
6 Dorsey (2012), Lin (2016).
7 Moore (2018).
8 Murphy (1999).
9 See Crisp (2017) for an overview.
10 Olson (2017).
11 Arvan (2016): 45–6, Smith (2013).
12 Pronin *et al.* (2008).
13 Pronin and Ross (2006): 204–5.
14 See also Morton (2013).
15 Aristotle [1984]: *Nicomachean Ethics*, Book I, $1098^{a}15$–20.
16 Haybron (2011): §1, Bruckner (2003): 34–5, Bricker (1980), Kant [1797]: 223, Price (2002), Pettigrew (forthcoming).
17 Bricker (1980), Bruckner (2003), Pettigrew (forthcoming).
18 Bruckner (2013), Dougherty (2015), Dorsey (2017, 2018).
19 Bruckner (2003): 34–5, Bricker (1980), Pettigrew (forthcoming), Price (2002).
20 Baumann (2018) argues that this is broader than Paul's (2015a, 2015b) problem of transformative experience, which I explore shortly.
21 Ullman-Margalit (2006), Briggs (2015). Cf. Paul (2015a, 2015b).
22 Baumann (2018): 264, Ullman-Margalit (2006).
23 Bykvist (2006).
24 Kahneman (2011): Chapter 38, Gilbert and Wilson (2009), Wilson and Gilbert (2003), Ayton *et al.* (2007).
25 Brickman *et al.* (1978), Myers and Diener (1995): 13, Argyle (1986).
26 Kahneman (2011), Lichtenstein and Slovic (1971), Grether and Plott (1979), Bazerman, *et al.* (1992).
27 Paul (2015a, 2015b).
28 Bykvist (2006), Paul (2015a), Pettigrew (2015, unpublished manuscript).
29 *The New American Bible* [2011]: Ecclesiastes, Chapter 9.
30 Ibid.: Wisdom of Ben Sira, especially Chapter 40. Also see Chapter 5: 11–15, Chapters 8–9, Chapter 11, Chapter 14, esp. 12–14, Chapter 18 esp. 22–26. Chapter 20.
31 Aurelius [1862]: especially Book IV, §8, Baltzly (2019): §5, Epictetus [1865]: *Enchiridion*.
32 Bruckner (2003).
33 Ibid.: §3. Cf. Rawls (1999a).
34 Rawls (1999a): §4.
35 Rawls (1999b): Part 1, §3.
36 Bruckner (2003): §§4–7.
37 Peterson (2017): §3.5.
38 Bruckner (2003): §8.
39 Bruckner (2003): 45.
40 Pettigrew (forthcoming), though see Isaacs (2019) for a critique.
41 In this and following sections where I argue prudence requires internalizing attitudes to 'moral risk-aversion', I mean merely that agents learn to avoid risking violating norms that *plausibly* (either from our perspective or theirs) appear to be 'moral', not that those norms *are* in fact moral in a normatively binding sense (viz. 'moral truths'). Instead, my argument will be that in internalizing attitudes against violating

social norms *plausibly* treated as 'moral' (Chapter 2), the prudent agent internalizes attitudes that can be used to derive what is *in fact* moral in a normatively binding sense (Chapter 3).
42 See, e.g. *Blow* (2001), *The Godfather Part II* (1974).
43 *Simmba* (2018).
44 See, e.g. *The Big Boss* (1971), *Kill Bill: Vol. 1* (2003).
45 *Star Wars*' (1977) character Han Solo is a paradigm case, along with many others.
46 *Thor* (2011).
47 Tucker (1991).
48 *Saved by the Bell* (1989a).
49 *Saved by the Bell* (1989b).
50 *Saved by the Bell* (1989c).
51 Baskin-Sommers *et al.* (2016).
52 Langone (2018).
53 Leiter (2015, 2018).
54 Ibid.
55 Leiter (2018).
56 Kochanska *et al.* (2002).
57 Kohlberg (1973).
58 Carpendale (2000).
59 Pettigrew (forthcoming).
60 Lewicka *et al.* (1992), Rozin and Royzman (2001), Ito *et al.* (1998), Baumeister *et al.* (2001). See also Kahneman and Tversky (1979).
61 Tom *et al.* (2007), Tversky and Kahneman (1992).
62 Samuelson and Zeckhauser (1988).
63 Morewedge and Giblin (2015)
64 Menegatti (2014).
65 Kahneman and Tversky (1984).
66 McNeil *et al.* (1988).
67 Bruckner (2003).
68 Pronin *et al.* (2008).
69 Herpertz and Sass (2000).
70 Van Gelder *et al.* (2013).
71 Baskin-Sommers *et al.* (2016).

References

Anand, P. (1995). *Foundations of Rational Choice under Risk*. Oxford: Oxford University Press.

Argyle, M. (1986). *The Psychology of Happiness*. London: Methuen.

Aristotle [1984]. *The Complete Works of Aristotle: The Revised Oxford Translation*. J. Barnes (Ed.). Princeton: Princeton University Press.

Arvan, M. (2016). *Rightness as Fairness: A Moral and Political Theory*. New York: Palgrave MacMillan.

Aurelius, M. [1862]. *Meditations*. G. Long (trans.). Logos Publishing, 2018.

Ayton, P., Pott, A., & Elwakili, N. (2007). Affective Forecasting: Why Can't People Predict Their Emotions? *Thinking & Reasoning*, *13*(1), 62–80.

Baltzly, D (2019). Stoicism. *The Stanford Encyclopedia of Philosophy*, E.N. Zalta (ed.), https://plato.stanford.edu/archives/spr2019/entries/stoicism/.

Baron, M. (1995). *Kantian Ethics Almost Without Apology*. Ithaca: Cornell University Press.

Baskin-Sommers, A., Stuppy-Sullivan, A.M., & Buckholtz, J.W. (2016). Psychopathic Individuals Exhibit but do not Avoid Regret during Counterfactual Decision Making. *Proceedings of the National Academy of Sciences, 113*(50), 14438–43.

Bazerman, M.H., Loewenstein, G.F., & White, S.B. (1992). Reversals of Preference in Allocation Decisions: Judging Alternatives versus Judging Among Alternatives. *Administrative Science Quarterly, 37*, 220–40.

Baumann, P. (2018). What Will Be Best for Me? Big Decisions and the Problem of Inter-World Comparisons. *Dialectica, 72*(2), 253–73.

Baumeister, R.F., Bratslavsky, E., Finkenauer, C., & Vohs, K.D. (2001). Bad is Stronger than Good. *Review of General Psychology, 5*(4), 323–70.

Blow (2001). https://www.imdb.com/title/tt0221027/, retrieved 29 July 2019.

Bricker, P. (1980). Prudence. *The Journal of Philosophy, 77*(7), 381–401.

Brickman, P., Coates, D., & Janoff-Bulman, R. (1978). Lottery Winners and Accident Victims: Is Happiness Relative? *Journal of Personality and Social Psychology, 36*(8), 917–27.

Broome, J. (2007). Does Rationality Consist in Responding Correctly to Reasons? *Journal of Moral Philosophy, 4*(3), 349–74.

Briggs, R. (2015). Transformative Experience and Interpersonal Utility Comparisons. *Res Philosophica, 92*, 189–216.

Bruckner, D.W. (2013) Present Desire Satisfaction and Past Well-Being. *Australasian Journal of Philosophy, 91*(1), 15–29.

——— (2003). A Contractarian Account of (Part of) Prudence. *American Philosophical Quarterly, 40*(1), 33–46.

Bykvist, K. (2006). Prudence for Changing Selves. *Utilitas, 18*(3), 264–83.

Carpendale, J.I. (2000). Kohlberg and Piaget on Stages and Moral Reasoning. *Developmental Review, 20*(2), 181–205.

Crisp, R (2017.). Well-Being. *The Stanford Encyclopedia of Philosophy*. E.N. Zalta (ed.), https://plato.stanford.edu/archives/fall2017/entries/well-being/.

Dorsey, D. (2018). Prudence and Past Selves. *Philosophical Studies, 175*(8), 1901–25.

——— (2017). Future-Bias: A Defense. *Pacific Philosophical Quarterly, 98*(S1), 351–73.

——— (2012). Subjectivism without Desire. *Philosophical Review, 121*(3), 407–42.

Dougherty, T. (2015). Future-Bias and Practical Reason. *Philosophers' Imprint, 15*(30), 1–16.

Epictetus [1865]. *The Complete Works of Epictetus*. E. Carter (Ed.). Cambridge: Little, Brown, and Company.

Gilbert, D.T. & Wilson, T.D. (2009). Why the Brain Talks to Itself: Sources of Error in Emotional Prediction. *Philosophical Transactions of the Royal Society B, 364,* 1335–41.

Grether, D.M. & Plott, C.R. (1979). Economic Theory of Choice and the Preference Reversal Phenomenon. *The American Economic Review, 69*(4), 623–38.

Hansson, S.O. (2005). *Decision Theory: A Brief Introduction,* https://people.kth.se/~soh/decisiontheory.pdf, retrieved 25 June 2018.

Haybron, D. (2011). Happiness. *The Stanford Encyclopedia of Philosophy.* E.N. Zalta (ed.), https://plato.stanford.edu/archives/fall2011/entries/happiness/.

Herpertz, S.C. & Sass, H. (2000). Emotional Deficiency and Psychopathy. *Behavioral Sciences & the Law, 18*(5), 567–80.

Isaacs, Y. (2019). The Problems of Transformative Experience. *Philosophical Studies* doi:10.1007/s11098-018-01235-3, 1–21.

Ito, T.A., Larsen, J.T., Smith, N.K., & Cacioppo, J.T. (1998). Negative Information Weighs More Heavily on the Brain: The Negativity Bias in Evaluative Categorizations. *Journal of Personality and Social Psychology, 75*(4), 887–900.

Kahneman, D. (2011). *Thinking Fast and Slow.* New York: Farrar, Straus, and Giroux.

Kahneman, D. & Tverksy, A. (1984). Choices, Values, and Frames. *American Psychologist, 39*(4), 341–50.

Kahneman, D. & Tversky, A. (1979). Prospect Theory: An Analysis of Decision under Risk. *Econometrica, 4,* 263–91.

Kant, I. [1797]. *The Metaphysics of Morals.* In M.J. Gregor (ed.), *The Cambridge Edition of the Works of Immanuel Kant: Practical Philosophy.* Cambridge: Cambridge University Press, 1996, 353–604.

——— [1788]. *Critique of Practical Reason,* in Ibid., 133–271.

——— [1785]. *Groundwork of the Metaphysics of Morals,* in Ibid., 38–108.

Kill Bill: Vol. 1 (2003). https://www.imdb.com/title/tt0266697/, retrieved 29 July 2019.

Kochanska, G., Gross, J.N., Lin, M.H., & Nichols, K.E. (2002). Guilt in Young Children: Development, Determinants, and Relations with a Broader System of Standards. *Child Development, 73,* 461–82.

Kohlberg, L. (1973). The Claim to Moral Adequacy of a Highest Stage of Moral Judgment. *The Journal of Philosophy, 70*(18), 630–46.

Korsgaard, C.M. (1996). *The Sources of Normativity.* New York: Cambridge University Press.

Lang, G. (2012). What's the Matter? Review of Derek Parfit, On What Matters. *Utilitas, 24*(2), 300–12.

Langone, A. (2018). #MeToo and Time's Up Founders Explain the Difference between the 2 Movements—and How They Are Alike. *Time.* http://time.com/5189945/whats-the-difference-between-the-metoo-and-times-up-movements/, retrieved 25 June 2018.

Leiter, B. (2018). The Disappearing Anonymous and Pseudonymous Blogs. *Leiter Reports*. http://leiterreports.typepad.com/blog/2018/05/the-disappearing-anonymous-and-pseudonymous-blogs.html, retrieved 25 June 2018.

―――― (2015). So What Happened to the 'Philosophy MetaMeta Blog', the Blog that...? *Leiter Reports*. http://leiterreports.typepad.com/blog/2015/01/so-what-happened-to-the-philosophy-metameta-blog-the-unmoderate-forum-that.html, retrieved 25 June 2018.

Lewicka, M., Czapinski, J., & Peeters, G. (1992). Positive-Negative Asymmetry or 'When the Heart Needs a reason'. *European Journal of Social Psychology*, *22*(5), 425–34.

Lichtenstein, S. & Slovic, P. (1971). Reversals of Preference between Bids and Choices in Gambling Decisions. *Journal of Experimental Psychology*, *89*, 46–55.

Lin, E. (2016). The Subjective List Theory of Well-Being. *Australasian Journal of Philosophy*, *94*(1), 99–114.

Lord, E. (2018). *The Importance of Being Rational*. Oxford: Oxford University Press.

McNeil, B.J., Pauker, S.G., & Tversky, A. (1988). On the Framing of Medical Decisions. In D.E. Bell, H. Raiffa, & A. Tversky (eds.), *Decision Making: Descriptive, Normative, and Prescriptive Interactions*. Cambridge: Cambridge University Press, 562–8.

Menegatti, M. (2014). New Results on the Relationship among Risk Aversion, Prudence and Temperance. *European Journal of Operational Research*, *232*(3), 613–7.

Moore, A. (2018). Hedonism. *The Stanford Encyclopedia of Philosophy*. E.N. Zalta (ed.), https://plato.stanford.edu/archives/win2018/entries/hedonism/.

Morewedge, C.K. & Giblin, C.E. (2015). Explanations of the Endowment Effect: An Integrative Review. *Trends in Cognitive Sciences*, *19*(6), 339–48.

Morton, J.M. (2013). Deliberating for Our Far Future Selves. *Ethical Theory and Moral Practice*, *16*(4), 809–28.

Murphy, M.C. (1999). The Simple Desire-Fulfillment Theory. *Noûs*, *33*(2), 247–72.

Myers, D.G. & Diener, E. (1995). Who is Happy? *Psychological Science*, *6*(1), 10–19.

Olson, E.T. (2017). Personal Identity. *The Stanford Encyclopedia of Philosophy*. E.N. Zalta (ed.), https://plato.stanford.edu/archives/sum2017/entries/identity-personal/.

Parfit, D. (2011). *On What Matters*, Vols. 1&2. Oxford: Oxford University Press.

―――― (2001). Rationality and Reasons. In D. Egonsson, J. Josefsson, B. Petersson, T. Ronnow-Rasmussen, & I. Persson (eds.), *Exploring Practical Philosophy: From Actions to Values*, Farmham: Ashgate, 17–39.

Paul, L.A. (2015a). *Transformative Experience*. Oxford: Oxford University Press.
―――― (2015b). What You Can't Expect When You're Expecting. *Res Philosophica*, 92(2), 1–23.
Peterson, M. (2017). *An Introduction to Decision Theory*, 2nd edition. Cambridge: Cambridge University Press.
Pettigrew, R. (forthcoming). *Choosing for Changing Selves*. Oxford University Press. https://philpapers.org/archive/PETCFC.pdf, retrieved 4 February 2019.
―――― (2015). Transformative Experience and Decision Theory. *Philosophy and Phenomenological Research*, 91(3), 766–74.
Price, B.W. (2002). The Worthwhileness Theory of the Prudentially Rational Life. *Journal of Philosophical Research*, 27, 619–39.
Pronin, E., Olivola, C.Y., & Kennedy, K.A. (2008). Doing Unto Future Selves as You Would Do Unto Others: Psychological Distance and Decision Making. *Personality and Social Psychology Bulletin*, 34(2), 224–36.
Pronin, E. & Ross, L. (2006). Temporal Differences in Trait Self-Ascription: When the Self is Seen as an Other. *Journal of Personality and Social Psychology*, 90(2), 197–209.
Rawls, J. (1999a). *A Theory of Justice: Revised Edition*. Cambridge, MA: The Belknap Press of Harvard University Press.
―――― (1999b). *The Law of Peoples, with 'The Idea of Public Reason Revisited'*. Cambridge, MA: Harvard University Press.
Rozin, P. & Royzman, E.B. (2001). Negativity Bias, Negativity Dominance, and Contagion. *Personality and Social Psychology Review*, 5(4), 296–320.
Samuelson, W. & Zeckhauser, R. (1988). Status Quo Bias in Decision Making. *Journal of Risk and Uncertainty*, 1(1), 7–59.
Saved by the Bell (1989a). The Lisa Card. https://www.imdb.com/title/tt0695233/, retrieved 5 June 2019.
―――― (1989b). The Gift. https://www.imdb.com/title/tt0695229/, retrieved 5 June 2019.
―――― (1989c). Fatal Distraction. https://www.imdb.com/title/tt0695193/, retrieved 5 June 2019.
Scanlon, T.M. (2014). *Being Realistic About Reasons*. Oxford: Oxford University Press.
Simmba (2018). https://www.imdb.com/title/tt7212726/, retrieved 5 June 2019.
Smith, M. (2017). Parfit's Mistaken Meta-ethics. In P. Singer (ed.), *Does Anything Really Matter?: Essays on Parfit and Objectivity*. Oxford: Oxford University Press, 99–120.
―――― (2013). A Constitutivist Theory of Reasons: Its Promise and Parts. *LEAP: Law, Ethics, and Philosophy*, 1, 9–30.
Star Wars (1977). Episode IV: A New Hope. https://www.imdb.com/title/tt0076759/, retrieved 5 June 2019.

Steele, K. & Stefánsson, H.O. (2016). Decision Theory. *The Stanford Encyclopedia of Philosophy.* E.N. Zalta (ed.), https://plato.stanford.edu/archives/win2016/entries/decision-theory/.
The Big Boss (1971). https://www.imdb.com/title/tt0067824/, retrieved 29 July 2019.
The Godfather Part II (1974). https://www.imdb.com/title/tt0071562/, retrieved 29 July 2019.
The New American Bible [2011]. Revised Edition. New Jersey: World Catholic Press.
Thor (2011). https://www.imdb.com/title/tt0800369/, retrieved 5 June 2019.
Tom, S.M. et al. (2007). The Neural Basis of Loss Aversion in Decision-making under Risk. *Science, 315*(5811), 515–8.
Tucker, K. (1991). Saved by the Bell. *Entertainment Weekly,* https://ew.com/article/1991/02/08/saved-bell/, retrieved 24 May 2019.
Tversky, A. & Kahneman, D. (1992). Advances in Prospect Theory: Cumulative Representation of Uncertainty. *Journal of Risk and Uncertainty, 5,* 297–323.
Ullmann-Margalit, E. (2006). Big Decisions: Opting, Converting, Drifting. *Royal Institute of Philosophy Supplements, 58,* 157–72.
Van Gelder, J.L., Hershfield, H.E., & Nordgren, L.F. (2013). Vividness of the Future Self Predicts Delinquency. *Psychological Science, 24*(6), 974–80.
Wilson, T.D. & Gilbert, D.T. (2003). Affective Forecasting. *Advances in Experimental Social Psychology, 35,* 345–411.
Wood, A. (2008). *Kantian Ethics.* Cambridge: Cambridge University Press.

3 Derivation of Morality from Prudence

I am far from the first to suggest that moral actions are prudent. As we have seen, this idea spans human history, from the teachings of major world religions, to ancient Western and non-Western philosophy, to common tropes in fiction, to how we typically raise our children and treat morality in our adult lives, and so on. However, Chapter 2's theory of prudence is novel. We saw that prudent individuals typically appear to internalize a specific form of *'moral risk-aversion'*: negative attitudes that treat immoral actions as risks categorically not worth taking due to the potential for severe regret, along with positive attitudes that treat moral actions as always having greater expected aggregate lifetime personal utility than immoral behavior. Chapter 2 theorized that prudent people tend to internalize these two sets of attitudes as standing constraints on first-order decision-making, thereby adopting a 'morally constrained utility-maximization' strategy in their everyday life decisions (see Figure 2.4).

This chapter argues that Chapter 2's theory of prudence entails a novel normative and descriptive theory of morality: a revised version of the theory I defended in *Rightness as Fairness: A Moral and Political Theory*. Section 3.1 provides an overview of Rightness as Fairness, along with a number of clarifying revisions. Section 3.2 then uses Chapter 2's theory of prudence to provide a new defense of Rightness as Fairness, showing how this book's theory of prudence can be used to defend the theory from a variety of criticisms. Finally, Section 3.3 shows how, when Chapter 2's theory of prudence is combined with this chapter's derivation of Rightness as Fairness, the result is a unified normative and descriptive neurofunctional theory of prudence, morality, and political morality.

1 *Rightness as Fairness*: An Overview

In *Rightness as Fairness*, I defended a broader psychological claim than I have here: namely, that virtually all of us (at least sometimes) want to know our future interests and weigh them against our interests in the present, so that we can be sure to act in ways we will not regret later.[1] Although I briefly drew connections between this claim and prudence,[2] I did not provide a detailed theory of prudence. Instead, I used a number of moral and non-moral cases to illustrate how we often appear to have these motives. Specifically, I argued that when the stakes of a decision seem high—such as when we are tempted to violate moral norms or are faced with a big life-decision (such as buying a home or getting married)—we sometimes want to know before making the decision whether we will regret it afterward.[3] I thought readers would find these cases persuasive. After all, people often talk about agonizing choices that 'keep us up at night', saying things such as, 'I wish I knew whether buying this home is the right choice', or 'I wish I knew whether I will regret lying to my boss'. Finally, I briefly suggested that these attitudes are prudent, as they keep us from making rash decisions such as buying a home on a whim or lying on impulse. The basic idea was that prudent people approach decisions with large stakes carefully, and with great forethought, in order to avoid decisions they might regret.[4]

I then argued that this kind of desire to know one's future interests generates a problem of diachronic instrumental rationality: the 'problem of possible future selves'—the problem of how an agent can possibly satisfy their desire to know their future interests before the future occurs.[5] I recognized that this problem is probably irresolvable in part, as the future can lead us to have involuntary and semi-voluntary interests (such as unexpected emotional reactions) that we cannot fully anticipate or control.[6] However, I then argued in Chapter 3 of *Rightness as Fairness* that it is possible for one's present and future selves to cooperate across time to partially resolve the problem, solving it as far as it can be. First, I argued that although one's present and future selves can both realize that one's present self cannot know which future will occur, both sets of selves can also realize that they each appear to have voluntary control over at least some of their interests: interests that they can *choose*.[7] Second, I argued that because both sets of selves can recognize that they can voluntarily choose at least some of their interests, it is possible and rational for one's present and future selves to forge and uphold a diachronic contract (across time) on voluntary interests to share with each other, given one's ignorance of the future in the present. Finally, I argued that the only contract that can achieve this is an agreement to act on voluntary interests that one's present and *every* possible future self can agree to share, regardless of how the future might turn out. This enables one's present self to act in ways they know will satisfy their voluntary future interests no matter how the future turns out, provided they choose in the future to uphold the contract. The principle representing this contract is as follows (clarifying revisions in italics):

> **The Categorical-Instrumental Imperative:** voluntarily aim for its own sake, in every relevant action,[8] to best satisfy the motivational interests it is instrumentally rational for one's present and every possible future self to universally agree upon given their other voluntary, involuntary, and semivoluntary interests and co-recognition of the problem of possible future selves, where relevant actions are determined recursively as actions it is instrumentally rational for one's present and possible future selves to universally agree upon as such when confronted by the problem of possible future selves—and then, when the future comes, voluntarily choose *to uphold* your having acted as such.[9]

On its face, this principle might seem implausible. First, it is very complex—which has led some to wonder how ordinary laypeople might understand or follow it.[10] Second, it may appear unclear why it is rational for one's present and future selves to forge and uphold such a contract, given how unlikely some of one's possible future selves are.[11] Third, it may seem unclear how one's future and every possible future self might arrive at such a universal agreement, given just how many possible future selves one has and the diversity of their potential interests.[12] Finally, several critics of *Rightness as Fairness* doubted the psychological claims the above argument is based upon. Why think that all of us sometimes want to know our future interests before the future occurs, so that we can avoid all possible regret?[13]

Shortly, I will argue that this book's theory of prudence helps resolve these issues. However, in order to do so, allow me to first present the rest of Rightness as Fairness as I previously defended it, along with some clarifying revisions.

1.1 The Categorical-Instrumental Imperative: Three Formulations

The Categorical-Instrumental Imperative holds that when one encounters the problem of possible future selves (viz. wanting to know one's future interests), one ought to act on voluntarily chosen interests that one's present and every possible future self can agree to share given their other interests. Let us now think about who one's possible future selves are. As Chapter 2 argued, prudent agents should regard their future as profoundly uncertain—as over the course of a complete life, one's life can turn in all kinds of unexpected directions. One related feature of human beings is that our involuntary and semi-voluntary inclinations to selfishness, other-regardingness, and altruism can change from moment to moment, week to week, or year to year. Nobody (besides Christ perhaps) always wants to behave altruistically. Sometimes—and science indicates it is more often than we might like to admit[14]—we are inclined to behave selfishly, often because of emotions that involuntarily or semi-voluntarily afflict us, such as anger or jealousy.[15] Conversely, we also sometimes have other-regarding interests, which may be rooted in emotions such as sympathy or compassion,[16] but also in reason.[17] Importantly, the extent to which we become more selfish, other-regarding, or altruistic may depend on our earlier choices and unexpected events. For example, a single choice in one's past—to pursue fame and career success over love—might alter the overall path of one's life to such an extent that, in one possible future, one becomes a narcissistic egoist, while in another possible future, one might have become more concerned for others.[18] Similarly, as St. Augustine's life famously illustrates, it is possible for a person to unexpectedly realize the error of their selfish ways, becoming a person committed to helping others.[19]

Because in different possible futures, one can involuntarily or semi-voluntarily end up with different levels of selfishness, other-regard, or even pure altruism, the Categorical-Instrumental Imperative requires one to act on voluntary interests that one's selfish and other-regarding possible future selves can voluntarily agree to share *despite* all of these possible differences. Consequently, the Categorical-Instrumental Imperative can be restated as follows (clarifying revisions in italics):

> **The Humanity-and-Sentience Formulation:** voluntarily aim for its own sake, in every relevant action, to best satisfy the motivational interests it is instrumentally rational for one's present

and every possible future self to universally agree upon given co-recognition that one's voluntary, involuntary, and semivoluntary interests *could be self-interested (viz. egoism)* or *concerned with the interests of other human or nonhuman sentient beings (viz. other-concern and altruism) along a vast continuum,* where relevant actions are determined recursively as actions it is instrumentally rational for one's present and possible future selves to universally agree upon as such in cases where one's present self wants to know and advance their future interests—and then, when the future comes, voluntarily choose to uphold your having acted as such.[20]

Now consider what such a universal agreement between one's present and every possible future self would involve. First, insofar as many of one's possible future selves care about their past—and many of one's possible past and future selves care in turn about their future—a truly universal agreement between one's present and every possible future self must be an agreement between every possible version of oneself one could possibly care about: past, present, and future. Such an agreement would, in other words, be a kind of 'categorical agreement': an agreement on how to act regardless of how the past or future might possibly turn out, and regardless of what one's interests in the past, present, or future could possibly be. Second, such an agreement would thus be one that advances the interests of one's egoistic possible selves but also the interests of one's other-regarding possible selves (including, as a limit-case, purely altruistic possible selves who care about the interests of all other human and nonhuman sentient beings equally).[21] Consequently, a truly universal agreement between one's present and every possible future self must strike a fair *intra*personal bargain between the interests of one's egoistic and other-regarding possible selves. Finally, to that extent, a universal agreement between all of one's possible selves will also constitute a fair *inter*personal bargain between one's own interests and the interests of other human and nonhuman sentient beings one might end up caring about. Consequently, I concluded that the Categorical-Instrumental Imperative requires acting in ways are fair to oneself (intrapersonally, to all of one's possible selves), where this is in turn identical to acting in ways that are fair to others (interpersonally, to all sentient beings). As a result, I concluded that the Categorical-Instrumental Imperative can thus be restated in a third way (clarifying revisions in italics):

The Kingdom-of-Human-and-Sentient-Ends Formulation: voluntarily aim for its own sake, in every relevant action, to abstract away from the interests (or ends) of particular human or nonhuman sentient beings, acting instead on interests (or ends) it is instrumentally rational for all human and nonhuman sentient beings to universally agree to share given their different voluntary, involuntary, and semivoluntary interests—*including any and every possible combination of egoistic and other-regarding desires different beings might have*—where relevant actions are determined recursively as actions it is instrumentally rational for one's present and possible future selves to universally agree upon as such in cases where one's present self wants to know and advance their future interests—and then, when the future comes, voluntarily choose to uphold your having acted as such.[22]

1.2 Comparison to Kantian Ethics

Notice how similar the three formulations of this principle are to Immanuel Kant's moral principle, the Categorical Imperative. Kant's first formulation of the Categorical Imperative holds that morality requires acting on maxims one can will to be universal laws of nature.[23] The first formulation of my Categorical-Instrumental Imperative is similar, entailing that morality requires acting in ways that all of one's own possible selves (and by extension, every other being they could care about) could universally agree upon. Kant's second formulation of the Categorical Imperative holds that we are to treat the humanity in ourselves and others as an end-in-itself.[24] Although the meaning of this formula remains debated,[25] my second formulation of the Categorical-Instrumental Imperative is similar but more inclusive. It requires one to act in ways that respect and advance the interests of oneself and every *sentient* being one could possibly care about, given their possible interests.[26] Finally, my third formulation of the Categorical-Instrumental Imperative, which requires seeking a consensus agreement between one's own interests and the interests of all possible sentient beings one could care about, is similar to but more inclusive than Kant's Kingdom of Ends formula, which holds only that morality is a matter of acting on principles that bring the ends of all *rational* beings into unity.[27]

My Categorical-Instrumental Imperative thus bears many similarities to Kantian ethics. However, there are a number of critical differences. First, my principle and its defense do not involve appeal to any special kind of imperative: namely, genuine categorical imperatives, or 'ought'-statements that are true without any condition.[28] Genuine categorical imperatives remain controversial.[29] My account does not deny that genuine categorical imperatives might be true. On the contrary, I argue elsewhere that if they are, they converge with the Categorical-Instrumental Imperative and Rightness as Fairness.[30] My account in *Rightness as Fairness* (and in the present book) merely holds that we can derive a robust form of 'categorical moral justification' from purely *instrumental* normative foundations.

This is important for a number of reasons. First, I contend it is an epistemically more certain foundation for moral philosophy. Whereas categorical normativity is controversial, virtually everyone (including children, criminals, and psychopaths) appears to recognize instrumental normativity.[31] Second, Rightness as Fairness appears more likely to motivate moral behavior than Kantianism, as my theory roots moral concern in mental time-travel, risk-aversion, and other-perspective-taking—all of which have all been consistently linked to moral cognition and moral motivation (see Chapter 1). Conversely, the motivational power of moral principles alone (*qua* Kantianism) has been empirically challenged.[32] Third, although some argue that Kantian ethics can include animals (through arguments similar to those in *Rightness as Fairness*[33]), my account includes animals more naturally, as my account roots morality itself in terms of what our possible future selves might end up caring about (including other creatures). Fourth, my account holds promise to unify a variety of competing moral frameworks—deontology, utilitarianism, contractualism, and virtue ethics—in a manner that Kantianism does not. As I will argue shortly, once we see that the Categorical-Instrumental Imperative is (typically) prudent for individuals, we can see that it also plausibly maximizes long-term expected social utility (viz. utilitarianism)—as it requires us to advance our own ends and the ends of others in a 'positive sum' manner via universal agreement (viz. contractualism). Further, as we will also see, the principles of fairness that I derive from the Categorical-Instrumental Imperative place constraints on how we can treat others (viz. deontology), while also requiring the development of standing dispositions of character to act on these principles (viz. virtue ethics). Consequently, this book's theory not only holds promise to unify prudence and morality but also the insights of four major moral frameworks.[34]

Derivation of Morality from Prudence 67

Finally, whereas Kant's formulas are thought to entail several different (and potentially divergent) moral tests,[35] my formulations of Categorical-Instrumental Imperative jointly entail a single moral test: a Moral Original Position. To see how, consider what it would be to act in ways that one's self and all possible human and nonhuman sentient beings could agree upon together, abstracting away from their differences (viz. my Kingdom-of-Human-and-Sentient-Ends Formula). John Rawls famously asks us to imagine all individuals in a given domestic society as represented behind a veil of ignorance,[36] a hypothetical device that precludes anyone from arbitrarily privileging themselves or their interests over others—which he then later extends to an international community of peoples.[37] Importantly, Rawls imposes a variety of stipulations on the original position, including that it only includes human beings[38] (in the first instance, representatives of citizens within a single domestic society assuming a closed society[39]), along with assumptions of reasonably favorable conditions,[40] strict-compliance with whichever principles are selected,[41] and a focus on major governmental institutions (viz. the 'basic structure' of society).[42] Many of these assumptions have been contested, with critics objecting to Rawls's strict-compliance assumption,[43] his anthropocentric focus on human beings,[44] his abstracting away from justice in families,[45] and focus on a closed society instead of a cosmopolitan concern for all human beings globally.[46]

My Categorical-Instrumental Imperative does not justify any of Rawls's controversial assumptions. The Categorical-Instrumental requires us to act in ways that all of our possible selves can agree upon *simpliciter*, irrespective of the conditions that they could possibly find themselves in, and irrespective of what they might possibly care about. Bearing this in mind, consider a Moral Original Position: a hypothetical situation where one deliberates from behind a veil of ignorance, but without any of Rawls's other controversial assumptions about justice.[47] In the Moral Original Position, we simply imagine a prudent agent behind a veil of ignorance whose task is to seek to advance their own interests, and the interests of every possible being they might end up caring about, without being able to bet on probabilities. This is what the Categorical-Instrumental Imperatives holds: that one should act on principles that *all* of their possible selves could accept as a consensus agreement, given all of the possible beings whose interests they might care about.

Although some critics have worried there is 'nothing moral' about the Moral Original Position, suggesting it is purely prudential and does not provide epistemic reasons to conform to whichever principles are rational from its standpoint,[48] we are now in a better position to understand precisely how the Moral Original Position is an epistemically justified moral model. First, we are epistemically justified in adopting the Moral Original Position—and in acting upon whichever principles are instrumentally rational from behind its veil of ignorance—to the extent that we have epistemic justification for believing that prudence normatively requires acting on the Categorical-Instrumental Imperative. I will provide this derivation shortly using Chapter 2's theory of prudence. Second, the Moral Original Position is a moral model insofar as it requires us to deliberate fairly about our own interests in relation to the interests of others. Its veil of ignorance not only requires us to care about the interests of all human and nonhuman sentient beings impartially, which is widely thought to be a defining feature of morality.[49] It also approximates Kant's influential notions of morality as universalizability[50] and of realizing a 'kingdom of ends', a harmony of ends arrived at via abstracting away from particular ends.[51] Although some readers may worry my account is still merely one of prudence (viz. instrumental rationality) rather than morality (viz. 'categorical imperatives'), Chapters 4 and 5 argue that principles of theory selection support reconceptualizing morality in these terms.

1.3 Four Principles of Fairness

Allow me to now summarize the Four Principles of Fairness that I derived from the Moral Original Position. In *Rightness as Fairness*, I argued that in the Moral Original Position, all one knows are general facts about sentience, interests, and agency.[52] First, one knows behind its veil of ignorance that all human and nonhuman sentient beings experience the world, having interests of their own. Second, one can recognize behind the veil that every being has higher-order interests: an interest in not having their first-order goals thwarted (viz. coercion), and an interest in receiving assistance when they cannot achieve their goals on their own and desire assistance (viz. mutual assistance). Because all human and nonhuman sentient beings have these two higher-order interests, I argued that it is rational to agree to at least two principles of fairness[53] from behind the Moral Original Position's veil of ignorance:

The Principle of Negative Fairness: all of our morally relevant actions should have as a guiding ideal, setting all costs aside, avoiding and minimizing coercion in all its forms (coercion resulting from intentional acts, natural forces, false beliefs, and so on), for all human and nonhuman sentient beings, for its own sake.

The Principle of Positive Fairness: all of our morally relevant actions should have as a guiding ideal, setting all costs aside, assisting all human and nonhuman sentient beings in achieving interests they cannot best achieve on their own and want assistance in achieving, for its own sake.[54]

I then argued, however, that these principles pose problems of costs and conflicts. First, the Principle of Negative Fairness can generate internal 'coercion conflicts'. In order to minimize coercion in the world, including what I have called natural coercion,[55] we sometimes need to coerce, as some degree of coercion (viz. police or military force) may be necessary to prevent greater amounts of coercion (viz. crimes or military invasion). Second, the Principles of Negative and Positive Fairness can conflict with each other. Sometimes the best means to help some is to coerce others (via taxation, etc.). Indeed, this is what libertarians and liberal-egalitarians disagree over in political philosophy: libertarians argue that it is wrong to coerce people to help others, whereas liberal-egalitarians think this is what justice requires.[56] Finally, the principles of Negative and Positive Fairness run up against issues of personal costs. Recall that although some of one's possible future selves may be altruistic—seeking to avoid coercing others and to help others selflessly—many of one's possible future selves are more self-interested, not wanting to bear particular costs for others' sake. This is often salient in discussions of applied ethics. For example, some theorists (such as Peter Singer) argue that people should be willing to endure great personal costs to help others in great need.[57] However, others argue such costs may require too much sacrifice for the sake of others.[58] The parties to the Moral Original Position should recognize these issues behind the veil. Specifically, although they possess *all-things-equal* grounds to avoid and minimize coercion (viz. Negative Fairness) and help others (viz. Positive Fairness), the various possible selves they might be also possess diverging interests in how to settle costs and conflicts generated by the Principles of Negative and Positive Fairness.

Consequently, I argued the parties to the Moral Original Position have rational grounds behind the veil to agree upon a third principle: a Principle of Fair Negotiation for reconciling conflicts within and between the Principles of Negative and Positive Fairness, and between the application of those principles and personal costs. The basic idea here is that negotiating a consensus compromise with others on how to apply the Principles of Negative and Positive Fairness is something that would advance one's own possible egoistic interests *and* the interests of any other human or nonhuman beings one could end up caring about. Although *Rightness as Fairness* could have been clearer about this, agents in the Moral Original Position should want fair negotiation to have a particular end: a consensus agreement between all those whom one's actions might affect (as again, the Categorical-Instrumental Imperative requires seeking universal agreement). *Rightness as Fairness* also could have been clearer about the nature of fair bargaining. Because the parties to the Moral Original Position are behind a veil ignorance—a situation in which they cannot arbitrarily favor any of their possible selves over others—they should want negotiated agreements not to arbitrarily favor anyone they might care about more above others. I will argue below that these clarifications have new and unexpected implications for Rightness as Fairness. For now, let us simply assume that it is rational for the parties to the Moral Original Position to agree upon the following principle for the above reasons (clarifying revisions in italics):

> **The Principle of Fair Negotiation:** whether an action is morally relevant, and how the Principles of Negative and Positive Fairness and Virtues of Fairness (see below) should be applied factoring in costs, should be settled *by a fairly negotiated agreement:* either an actual agreement predicated upon all human and nonhuman sentient beings potentially affected by the action *being motivated by the above principles but lacking any arbitrary bargaining advantages or disadvantages, or to the extent that such an actual agreement is infeasible (including because nonhuman beings affected may not be able to negotiate given their capacities),* through a hypothetical process approximating the same, for its own sake.[59]

Notice that this principle does not preclude negotiating agents from taking into account real-world probabilities. The *Categorical-*

Instrumental Imperative holds that morality is a matter of acting on principles that all of one's possible future selves can agree upon without betting on probabilities. The Moral Original Position then represents this rational requirement through its veil of ignorance, which prevents the agent from favoring any of their possible future selves over any others on the basis of probabilities. The Principle of Fair Negotiation, on the other hand, is an *outcome* of a rational agent's deliberations from behind the veil—and my contention here is that one's present and all of one's possible future selves can *agree* to this principle letting real-world agents negotiate on the basis of probabilities. In brief, all of one's selves can recognize that real-world choosers must take into probabilities when weighing the Principles of Negative and Positive Fairness against costs, since all of one's possible selves live in an uncertain world where choosing on the basis of probabilities cannot ultimately be avoided. This is important because the Principle of Fair Negotiation thus permits fair (moral) negotiation to incorporate our preferences for 'special relationships'—for the people (friends, family-members, fellow citizens, and so on) we ordinarily take ourselves to be more likely to care about (and care about more), compared to complete strangers. All the Principle of Fair Negotiation requires is that one does not act in ways that *unfairly* neglect anyone in negotiation, including complete strangers—as the Categorical-Instrumental Imperative requires us to recognize that it is possible for our future selves to unexpectedly care about strangers.[60] This account, I believe, is highly intuitive: morality does permit us to negotiate norms that protect and prioritize special relationships. It simply requires that we do so in ways that are not unfair to others and which we *might* regret later.

Next, I argued that individuals in the Moral Original Position have rational grounds to agree upon a fourth principle: a principle of virtue that requires developing standing psychological dispositions to act on the other principles just arrived at:

> **The Principle of Virtues of Fairness:** all of our morally relevant actions should aim to develop and express stable character traits to act in accordance with the first three principles of fairness, for its own sake.[61]

Further, insofar as things like recognizing and addressing coercion, recognizing and helping people and animals in need, and negotiating fairly with others are all skills, this principle implicitly involves cultivating such skills.[62]

72 Derivation of Morality from Prudence

Finally, I combined these Four Principles of Fairness into a single criterion of moral rightness, which I now simplify and revise as follows to reflect the clarifying revisions above:

> **Rightness as Fairness:** an action is morally right if and only if it is morally relevant and *pursues or conforms to a fairly negotiated agreement*, where such an agreement is the result of all human and nonhuman sentient beings potentially affected by the action either actually negotiating with each other in conformity with the Four Principles of Fairness, or else through a hypothetical process approximating the same, for its own sake; where, finally, moral relevance is determined recursively by the Four Principles of Fairness (coercion, mutual assistance, fair bargaining, and virtues of fairness demarcating morally-relevant cases).[63]

This criterion is admittedly complex—so much so that some readers might wonder whether it can possibly be correct. However, we will soon see that its complexities in fact appear to be borne out in how ordinary people think about morality, particularly the role that negotiation plays in social-political theory and social justice activism.

2 Rightness as Fairness: A Revised Defense

Critics of *Rightness as Fairness* questioned several of the claims summarized above. I will now argue that this book's theory of prudence can be used to defend Rightness as Fairness against these concerns in a manner that leads the theory in important new directions.

2.1 A Revised Defense of Rightness as Fairness's Moral Psychology

One common objection to *Rightness as Fairness* was that it is unclear whether all people at least sometimes have the motivations that produce the 'problem of possible future selves': namely, a desire to know one's own future interests.[64] However, Chapter 2 defended a much more qualified claim: that *prudent* people typically want to avoid regret in morally salient cases, wanting to make (moral) choices they know they will not regret (Figure 2.5).

Several points here are important. First, if my argument in Chapter 2 is correct, then critics may have been correct in that not everyone may have the kinds of motivational interests that make Rightness as Fairness rational. Indeed, as Chapter 5 examines, there may be people who lack these motives. Chapter 2's point was more qualified: namely, that prudent people typically have motives that generate the 'problem of possible future selves', as well as an overall moral-prudential psychology that I argue below can be used to provide a newer, better derivation of Rightness as Fairness. Further, although I argued in Chapter 2 that 'moral risk-aversion' typically appears to be prudent, given life's many uncertainties and particular empirical regularities, Chapter 5 will discuss the possibility of (hopefully rare) counterexamples: individuals who can act prudently without moral risk-aversion, and for whom Rightness as Fairness may thus be irrational.

To some readers, it might seem unacceptable for a theory to contend that morality may not always be rational. However, two central points of this book (to be defended in Chapters 4 and 5) are that (1) we should select theories on the basis of rigorous principles of theory selection, and (2) this book's theory satisfies such principles across a wide variety of normative and descriptive phenomena better than alternative theories of morality and moral psychology. Consequently, my response to *Rightness as Fairness*'s prior critics is twofold. First, this book provides better normative foundations for the theory. Whereas *Rightness as Fairness* defended the overly-ambitious claim that virtually everyone has motivations that make its principles rational, Chapter 2 argued merely that prudence *typically* requires these attitudes—an argument further supported below in Sections 3.2.2 and 3.2.3. Second, I think we should take seriously the (admittedly disturbing) possibility that morality may not always be normatively binding, for precisely the reasons this book's theory identifies. For as Chapter 5 argues, some normative philosophical thought-experiments and empirical research both suggest that morality may not always be normatively binding—though I leave these matters for further inquiry.

2.2 A Revised Derivation of the Categorical-Instrumental Imperative

In *Rightness as Fairness*, I provided two derivations of the Categorical-Instrumental Imperative. The first derivation was direct. In cases where one's dominant motive is to know one's future interests, I argued there is only one way to satisfy this interest: one's

74 Derivation of Morality from Prudence

present and possible future selves must agree with one another on voluntary interests to share across time given the inability of one's present self to know which future self one will be.[65] I also provided a second derivation using decision-theory and the mathematics of infinity, as I argued we have an infinite variety of possible future selves.[66] Richard Dees argued that both derivations are unsuccessful, contending that I must show that the expected long-term value of moral action is greater than immoral action.[67] I will now address this concern.

To see how this book's theory of prudence can be used to show that the expected value of conforming to the Categorical-Instrumental Imperative is at least typically greater than alternatives, consider again the two moral-prudential lessons examined in Chapter 2. Chapter 2 argued that prudent individuals typically internalize 'morally risk-averse' attitudes: beliefs and desires that (1) immorality is not worth the risk of immense regret, and (2) morality has greater-expected personal outcomes in the long-term, at least if you are patient. As we have seen in this chapter, the first of these attitudes gives rise to the problem of possible future selves. In morally salient cases, the prudent agent does not want to risk outcomes their future selves might profoundly regret. Instead, they want to make a choice they know they will not regret. The direct derivation of the Categorical-Instrumental Imperative in *Rightness as Fairness* (the derivation not involving infinite expected utilities) showed that the only way to satisfy this negative motive is for one's present and possible future selves to universally agree on voluntary interests to share for their own sake, irrespective of what the future holds. The rest of *Rightness Fairness*—the derivation of the three formulations of the Categorical Instrumental Imperative, the derivation of the Moral Original Position as a moral test, and the Four Principles of Fairness—were then shown to be the only principles that achieve that kind of agreement. Consequently, the Categorical-Instrumental Imperative and moral content of Rightness as Fairness can be derived from this book's account of prudent individuals' internalized categorical negative attitudes that *violating moral norms is never worth the risk of immense regret*.

However, this is only half of the story we can now tell. The next question then becomes why satisfying this negative motive (viz. conformity to Categorical-Instrumental Imperative) is instrumentally rational. *Rightness as Fairness* argued that this can be established through the mathematics of infinity. However, we

Derivation of Morality from Prudence 75

can now see that the answer is more straightforward. Chapter 2 argued that prudent agents also typically internalize a positive set of categorical attitudes—attitudes that *morality always has better likely personal outcomes than immorality in the long-term*, at least if you are patient. Dees's challenge was that my instrumental derivation of the Categorical-Instrumental Imperative succeeds if and only if the expected value of acting according to it is higher than other alternatives. This book has not provided a proof of this. Instead, it has defended a narrower thesis: that *in real life, given various empirical regularities*, prudent people typically internalize attitudes which entail—for them, given their morally risk-averse attitudes—that adherence to the Categorical-Instrumental Imperative maximizes expected aggregate lifetime personal utility. If this is correct, then it is typically prudent to be the kind of person whose attitudes make it rational to obey the Categorical-Instrumental Imperative and the moral theory (Rightness as Fairness) that principle entails.

Some readers may consider this a serious capitulation, as it amounts to recognizing that the Categorical-Instrumental Imperative (and Rightness as Fairness) may not always be rational. However, my response to this concern is four-fold. First, proof that morality is always rational is a bar that no moral theory has ever clearly met (which is why there is still so much controversy over these issues[68]). Second, this book's theory of prudence identifies the rationality of morality as an empirical issue: namely, whether, and to what extent, moral risk-aversion (as I defended it) is rational for different individuals in different contexts. As we will see in Chapter 5, I believe this is a very important question for future research to pursue. Third, there are further reasons for optimism about morality's rationality, as recent empirical work suggests that moral behavior is beneficial for individuals' physical and psychological well-being across the human life span, from childhood through later life.[69] Finally, this book's theory of prudence provides an intuitive model of how moral behavior is typically a prudent long-term strategy.

We can see how plausible its account is by considering real-life cases. Consider wanton 'immoralists': the common criminal, hitman, mob boss, political dictator, and so on. Although individuals like these can get away with and benefit from immoral behavior, there are grounds for thinking that their willing to risk immoral behavior tends to be an imprudent life-strategy, at least in the long-run. Criminals tend to end up in trouble with the law, often ending up in prison. Similarly, many political dictators throughout history (ranging from Adolf Hitler to Saddam Hussein, Muammar al-Gaddafi, and so on) have ended up deposed or killed. Finally, in the course of everyday life, although people sometimes seemingly get away with immoral behavior 'scot-free', we have repeatedly seen ourselves or others face severe social sanctions for immoral behavior, such as divorces for infidelity to loss of jobs for deception, and so on. Sometimes, as in the case of the #MeToo movement's allegations of sexual misconduct, we see people suffer profoundly negative consequences for immoral behavior committed many years earlier. For all of these reasons, prudent individuals typically learn to not be these kinds of individuals: to not be individuals willing to risk immoral behavior for personal gain. Prudent people like you and I have seen the regrets immoral behavior tends to give rise to—so we internalize dispositions to not risk such immense regrets, instead aiming to behave morally 'for its own sake'. We come to believe that morality is a better life-policy than immorality and want to behave morally rather than immorally.

Are there potential counterexamples—individuals for whom moral risk-aversion is not required by prudence? Perhaps. First, there may be 'high-stakes' counterexamples: cases of political dictators or business leaders who never suffer for their moral crimes. Second, there may be 'low-stakes' counterexamples: cases where people routinely get away with more minor moral infractions, such never returning favors, cutting in line, and so on. This book cannot refute all of these potential counterexamples, nor do I think it should. Although proof that morality is always rational is arguably the 'holy grail' of moral philosophy, no such proof is widely accepted. I now believe this is for good reason. For as Chapter 5 discusses, I believe the rationality of morality is an empirical issue. Chapter 2 merely suggested that you, I, and most other everyday prudent people tend to learn over time to treat immoral actions as not worth the risk, and to internalize attitudes that morality has greater long-term expected benefit. I believe Chapter 2 made a compelling case for this, and Chapter 4 will argue that this book's overall theory coheres well with behavioral neuroscience. At the same time, I will recognize in Chapter 5 that it is an empirical question how far my account of prudence generalizes, and hence, whether morality (*qua* Rightness as Fairness) always is rational. I will now move on to Dees's next objection.

2.3 Defending Rightness as Fairness's *(Revised)* Principles of Fairness

Dees also called into question *Rightness as Fairness*'s account of fair negotiation, its Four Principles of Fairness, and standard of moral rightness. Here again, I think there is much to learn.

2.3.1 Clarifying the Instrumental Value of Fair Negotiation

Dees's first concern about the content of Rightness as Fairness is that it is unclear what instrumental value negotiating with other people has (viz. the Principle of Fair Negotiation), and how negotiating with other people amounts to negotiating agreements between our own possible future selves.[70] We can now see how this book's account of prudence can help us understand the instrumental value of negotiating agreements fairly (viz. ideals of coercion-minimization, mutual assistance, and fair bargaining), as well as how negotiating agreements with others is akin to negotiating agreements between our own future selves.

As Chapter 2 argued, prudent individuals typically internalize the desire to avoid outcomes they might profoundly regret. This means that they want to act in ways that make as many of their possible future selves happy with their decisions as possible—in the limit, all of them. Now consider the possible future selves one has. Some of one's possible future selves may be relatively selfish, caring about their own interests to the exclusion of others' interests. However, other possible future selves are more strongly altruistic, caring about other people's (and other creatures') interests over their own. *Betting* on any of these selves is an inherently risky endeavor. We see this in the case of criminals, and most powerfully in morally and prudentially tragic cases such as Hitler, Nazism, the Holocaust, and World War II. Criminals bet on their selfish future selves, not caring about how they harm others. The problem for criminals, however, is that other people do not typically enjoy being treated unfairly. For notice again what tends to happen, at least as a broad empirical regularity, to immoralists including everyday criminals, spouses guilty of infidelity, people who cheat on exams, slaveholders, and dictators such as Hitler. They are typically (though again, not always) *punished* for their unfair behavior, at least in the longer run: criminals tend to end up in jail, cheating spouses are often found out and divorced, exam-cheaters often receive failing grades and academic suspensions, political dictators often end up dead or imprisoned, and so on.

Is it possible to commit immoral acts and never suffer severe consequences? Perhaps. Again, some people may indeed get away with immoral behavior in perpetuity. However, these individuals appear to be outliers. The vast majority of us typically learn across childhood, adolescence, and adulthood that immorality is a bad bet in an uncertain world. Conversely, why should we think that negotiating fair compromises with others is (instrumentally) a good bet? The answer again has to do with one's possible future selves. As Chapter 2 argued, prudent individuals have internalized attitudes that make them want to act, in morally salient cases, in ways they will not regret (Figure 2.5). On my account, it is this motive that generates the 'problem of possible future selves': the problem of how to *know* one's future interests before the future occurs. I argue only the Categorical-Instrumental Imperative resolves this problem.

Bearing this in mind, consider the ways one's future selves can end up regretting one's actions in the present. One way one can end up regretting one's actions is by behaving immorally, as this can result in social punishment or guilt. However, another way one can end up regretting one's actions is by sacrificing an unfair amount for others. Sometimes, when we give others more than is fair, we involuntarily or semivoluntarily end up feeling resentful, such as when we help friends who never help in return, or try to do nice things for others only to have them treat us 'like a doormat'. Because some of one's possible future selves are more selfish and others more altruistic, betting firmly on one set of selves over the others is a serious risk. The Categorical-Instrumental Imperative holds that the only instrumentally rational response to these possibilities is to act in ways that one's selfish and altruistic future selves can agree upon *despite* their differences—so that one's future selves will not regret one's actions in the present no matter how the future goes. Furthermore, I argue that this is precisely what fairly negotiated agreements accomplish. When you and I negotiate a fair agreement, we act in ways that advance our own egoistic interests while also advancing the interests of the other person—a person who our future selves might end up caring about, either for self-interested reasons (if you object to how I treated you and retaliate) or due to empathy. Conversely, when we fail to negotiate fair agreements with others, we run serious risks: risks of treating others in ways that they object to and punish us for, or ways that involve us sacrificing so much that we regret it because our future selves judge we sacrificed 'too much'. Negotiated agreements enable one to act in ways such that one's future self can advance their interests without feeling like they sacrificed excessively.

I believe this is an intuitive idea. If I fail to negotiate fairly with you, treating you the way I (unilaterally) think is best, then you may object and seek to punish me for failing to care sufficiently for your interests as you understand them. Conversely, if you fail to negotiate fairly with me, then you may treat *me* in ways I think are unfair or expect too much. It is only by arriving at and upholding a fair agreement that we can both be sure to advance our interests, whether they are more self-concerned (viz. egoism) or other-concerned (viz. altruism).

Finally, we can see the *disvalue* of failure to negotiate fairly by considering cases involving individuals or groups. Consider two spouses who disagree over how to raise their child. If one spouse insists upon their way, coercing the other spouse to go along with them, the other spouse may become resentful, blaming them for every bad decision the child makes and sparking constant arguments. And indeed, fairness violations generally appear to stimulate retribution.[71] Conversely, if the two spouses *fairly negotiate an agreement*, then they can raise the child in harmony, according to an agreement that both sides perceive as fair. Further, if the child-rearing strategy they agree upon appears to fall short of their mutual satisfaction, they can fairly renegotiate a new strategy. Similar considerations plausibly apply to groups, including nations. When one group treats another unfairly, abusing bargaining advantages to coerce the other group—as in slavery, racism, sexism, and so on—the dominated group may be (rightly) inclined to seek retribution. Further, although retribution may be impossible or ineffective in the short-term, it can *become* effective as time goes on—as illustrated by many social conflicts, ranging from the US Civil War to the Israeli-Palestinian conflict, and so on. Yet retribution and counter-retribution are plausibly in no one's interest. As historian and onetime US Diplomat to Germany William Dodd once said, 'It would be no sin if statesmen learned enough of history to realize that no system that implies control of society by privilege seekers has ended in any other way than collapse'.[72] It is only by fairly negotiating agreements with others, both individually and collectively, that we are able to realize a future that advances our own interests and the interests of others we *might* end up caring about.

80 *Derivation of Morality from Prudence*

As such, I believe Dees's concerns about the instrumental rationality of fair negotiation can be provisionally met. First, fairly negotiating with others appears to typically be instrumentally optimal given uncertainty about the future. Second, negotiating fairly with others is 'negotiating with one's future selves' in the sense that fairly negotiated agreements with other individuals and groups preserve the ability of one's own future selves to pursue their own goals and the goals of others they might end up caring about. However, Chapter 5 will explore the possibility that Rightness as Fairness (and hence, fair negotiation) is not always rational, ultimately leaving these as important empirical questions to be answered by future research.

2.3.2 Clarifying Coercion-Minimization, Mutual Assistance, and Fair Bargaining

Dees's second concern about the content of Rightness as Fairness concerns the *nature* of fair negotiation. First, Dees writes:

> [E]ven if we accept that the principle requires actual negotiations between separate people, approximating equal bargaining power only makes sense if we already know what counts as the requisite form of equality. But equality is a morally loaded notion, which is supposed to be the *product* of the negotiations.[73]

Second, Dees writes:

> ...Arvan takes the actual negotiation clause very seriously, citing it as one of the great advantages of his view.... But to avoid the obvious problems with forcing people to negotiate for basic rights, he concedes that we do not need to negotiate with people who do not share a commitment to basic equality and to his principles of non-coercion and assistance to others (182–84). He somehow misses the fact that the most contentious debates—those about abortion, women's rights, LGBTQI rights, and even about welfare rights—are mostly about what is required to treat people equally and without coercion. On his grounds, then, these debates are not ones open to negotiations, but he thereby undermines the centrality of actual negotiations that are the hallmark of his theory.[74]

I argue that Chapter 2's account of prudence, and the revisions made to Rightness as Fairness in this chapter, resolve these problems in ways that lead the theory in important new directions.

I believe Dees is right: coercion-minimization, mutual assistance, and equal bargaining are all moralized notions. Abortion-opponents think abortion restrictions minimize coercion by protecting fetuses from death. Defenders of abortion rights, however, think abortion restrictions unfairly coerce women. And so on (for LGBTQIA+ rights, etc.). Let us think, then, about how a prudent individual—one who faces the problem of possible future selves—should consider this problem. Here the very same problem of uncertainty underlying Chapter 2's account of prudence recurs. Consider an anti-abortion activist or politician who opposes LGBTQIA+ rights. It may seem like a 'good bet' for this person (for instance, based on their personal religious convictions) to seek to impose their moral views on others—passing laws against abortion or LGBTQIA+ rights. However, what if—entirely unexpectedly—they come to have a family member who these policies would negatively impact? For example, what if, after passing an anti-abortion law, a politician has a daughter who loses her life seeking an illegal abortion? Or, what if, after passing a law against gay marriage, a politician learns their child is gay? In both cases, the person's moral beliefs and preferences may radically change—and indeed, there are notable cases in which people's moral views and preferences unexpectedly changed for precisely these kinds of reasons.[75] Do some people stick to their moral beliefs on particular issues (e.g. LGBTQIA+ rights) even after having a personal experience that challenges said belief? Almost certainly. The question, though, is whether it is rational to bet that one's moral beliefs on controversial issues will not change in an uncertain world. This is less obvious, given that people's beliefs often do seem to change over time and in unexpected ways. For example, cultural attitudes toward LGBTQIA+ issues changed quickly and dramatically in the US,[76] as they have for many other social moral issues, such as the morality of marijuana legalization,[77] the morality of particular wars,[78] and abortion.[79] If this book is correct, a prudent person should thus not assume that their beliefs and preferences on controversial moral issues will remain the same. They should instead recognize that life is profoundly uncertain over the long-term, and that their moral views on contentious moral issues *might* change over time in unpredictable ways.

82 Derivation of Morality from Prudence

Let us suppose, then, that prudent individuals will agree to Rightness as Fairness's principles (via my previous arguments), but also know that their own views and preferences about how to interpret and apply these principles might change dramatically over time. What should they then do? They should seek a *decision-procedure* that addresses that problem—one settling how people who are committed to ideals of coercion-minimization, mutual assistance, and fair (nonarbitrary) bargaining power should respond to the fact that their own views might change over time. Is there such a model? Indeed, there is: a series of Rawlsian Social-Political Original Positions.

To see how, consider the grounds that Rawls gives for the original position as a model of justice. Rawls supposes that the model represents citizens who (A) are committed to cooperating fairly for mutual advantage but (B) disagree over exactly what fairness involves, and also (C) recognize that their own views and preferences might change over time. In such a model, what is it to be committed to cooperating fairly for mutual advantage? As Rawls himself delineates, every person in the original position wants to advance their own preferences: they do not want to be coercively prevented from achieving things they want, and they may want to be helped by others (i.e. society) in pursuing their goals. The veil of ignorance then ensures that no one has arbitrary bargaining power over anyone else. Finally, the veil of ignorance requires the parties to recognize that their own preferences might change over time. Rawls's original position thus represents *all* of the preferences and uncertainty about the future that instrumentally rational agents should arrive at via the Moral Original Position. It models people committed to coercion-minimization (Negative Fairness), mutual assistance (Positive Fairness), nonarbitrary bargaining (Fair Negotiation), and the development of a standing sense of fairness (Virtues as Fairness).

Consequently, Rightness as Fairness should not be seen as entailing that its Four Principles of Fairness directly specify what is right or wrong for any situation or issue (e.g. abortion, global poverty). Rather, this book's theory of prudence can be seen as entailing a Prudential Original Position for deriving principles of prudence, a Moral Original Position for deriving moral principles, and a series of *Social-Political Original Positions* for interpreting and applying Rightness as Fairness under different possible social and political conditions, as people's views and preferences emerge or change over time. Allow me to explain.

2.3.3 Revising Rightness as Fairness's Content as a Moral and Political Theory

Dees's final critique is that I did not adequately circumscribe the moral limits of negotiation:

> Arvan emphasizes negotiations because he rightly observes that most human interactions are negotiated as we go.... But in practice the real-life negotiations that he promotes are either mere exercises in power or they are bounded by moral rules, rules that must be in place *before* the negotiations begin.[80]

Dees's concerns here are justified and have led me to see that Rightness as Fairness—as I previously developed it—is incomplete.

First, although Dees is correct that people rarely have equal/ nonarbitrary bargaining power in real life, in many cases we do *approximate* it. We approximate equal bargaining power, for example, in friendships and relationships among equals, such as in marriages where neither spouse exploits unfair bargaining power over the other (such as financial power). In these cases, I think it is entirely intuitive to say that morality is the result of actual negotiation: in relationships among equals, the equal parties settle the moral terms of their interactions through forging and upholding fair agreements with each other.

Second, notice that there is an increasing realization in social and political theory that this is what justice requires more generally: eliminating arbitrary bargaining advantages. For example, consider evolving standards of consent in sexual relationships. One emerging ideal is that of equal bargaining power, such that the requirement not to abuse power is a requirement on consent itself. Similarly, consider conversations about white privilege: here, too, the idea is that it is wrong and unjust to not help those who have been (or are currently) oppressed, given one's own greater bargaining power as a white person. In other words, it is increasingly recognized that in order for our individual actions to be moral (viz. not wrongly coercing others through unfair bargaining power), social and political mechanisms must be in place to ensure there are no arbitrary inequalities in bargaining power.

Notice what this suggests. Rawls wrote in *A Theory of Justice* that the model of justice as fairness he presents is one that a certain kind of person will find attractive: people who live in modern-democratic conditions. Why? I think we see the answer in the trends just mentioned. Many (though by no means all) people in modern democracies have, to a greater or lesser extent, *internalized* Rightness as Fairness's norms of fairness: ideals of non-coercion (e.g. free speech), mutual assistance (e.g. social security), and view that arbitrary bargaining advantages are unfair (no one should be disadvantaged on the basis of race, gender, etc.). More importantly, if this book is correct, there is a deeper truth here: namely, that *prudent* people will have these motives, wanting to organize their society on fair grounds—grounds that aim to reduce coercion, assist each other, and realize nonarbitrary bargaining power over contested issues (viz. Rightness as Fairness).

We can now see that Rawls gave us a model of exactly this: a model of free and equal individuals seeking to apply Rightness as Fairness to social-political conditions. By representing every individual in society behind a veil of ignorance, every party to the original position is given (A) an equal, nonarbitrary say over the extent to which they are (B) free from coercion and (C) able to seek and receive assistance by others—which is what Rightness as Fairness's Four Principles of Fairness entitle everyone to. Hence, Rawlsian Social-Political Original Positions *just are* models of what Rightness as Fairness requires, viz. prudence and morality. But there are further implications. If, as I argued previously, prudence and morality are a matter of acting in ways that treat one's future self as though their interests could be identical to any possible human or nonhuman sentient beings, agents motivated by Rightness as Fairness should want to realize a fair *world*: a world that treats every person and nonhuman sentient being they might care about as fairly as possible, including future generations. This suggests that prudence—which in the broadest sense means realizing a world that is rational for one's future selves, given life's uncertainty—requires settling how to apply Rightness as Fairness through a Cosmopolitan Original Position, which is something Rawls's cosmopolitan critics have long maintained.[81]

If this is correct, then Rightness as Fairness is not the end of social-political theory or applied ethics: it is the beginning. Prudence is a matter of acting on principles that are rational from a Prudential Original Position, morality is a matter of acting on principles (Rightness as Fairness) that are rational from a Moral

Original Position, and interpreting and applying Rightness as Fairness requires adopting a series of Social-Political Original Positions—beginning with a Cosmopolitan Original Position that includes all persons and sentient beings as *entitled to fairness*. Allow me to elaborate.

First, there is a question of which principles individuals in a Cosmopolitan Original Position would agree to at the level of ideal theory, that is, for defining a world in which all persons and sentient beings would be treated fairly. Many have suggested these principles are ones that would afford every human being in the world equal rights and liberties, fair equality of opportunity, and maximize the income and wealth of the world's global poor[82]—and others have argued for including animals in Rawlsian original positions.[83] However, another possibility is that individuals in a Cosmopolitan Original Position would recognize the importance of nation-states. In that case, it might be rational for individuals in the Cosmopolitan Original Position to agree to adopt an International Original Position to model fairness to nation-states of the sort Rawls defended in *The Law of Peoples*.[84] Next, individuals in a Cosmopolitan Original Position plausibly have grounds to seek an agreement on what fairness requires within nation-states—which would require them to adopt a Domestic Original Position of the sort Rawls defended in *A Theory of Justice* and *Political Liberalism*.[85]

Finally, individuals at each level should be concerned not only with understanding what Rightness as Fairness requires under ideal conditions (viz. assumptions of strict-compliance), but also how to interpret and apply Rightness as Fairness's principles fairly in our presently unfair world. In recent work, I have argued that this is best understood in terms of another type of iteration of the original position: a Nonideal Original Position that can be adapted to different kinds of unfair conditions (global unfairness, unfairness in modern-democracies, etc.) to specify what is fair in a given social-political domain given unfairness.[86] Although this work is still in its early stages, I have suggested that the Nonideal Original Position results in a variety of plausible principles for redressing injustice and unequal bargaining power.

The result we have ended up at is this. Some philosophers have criticized Rawls's outsized influence on modern political philosophy—arguing that Rawls's overall approach to theorizing about justice is misguided.[87] Our conclusions here, however, suggest otherwise. If this book's theory of prudence and

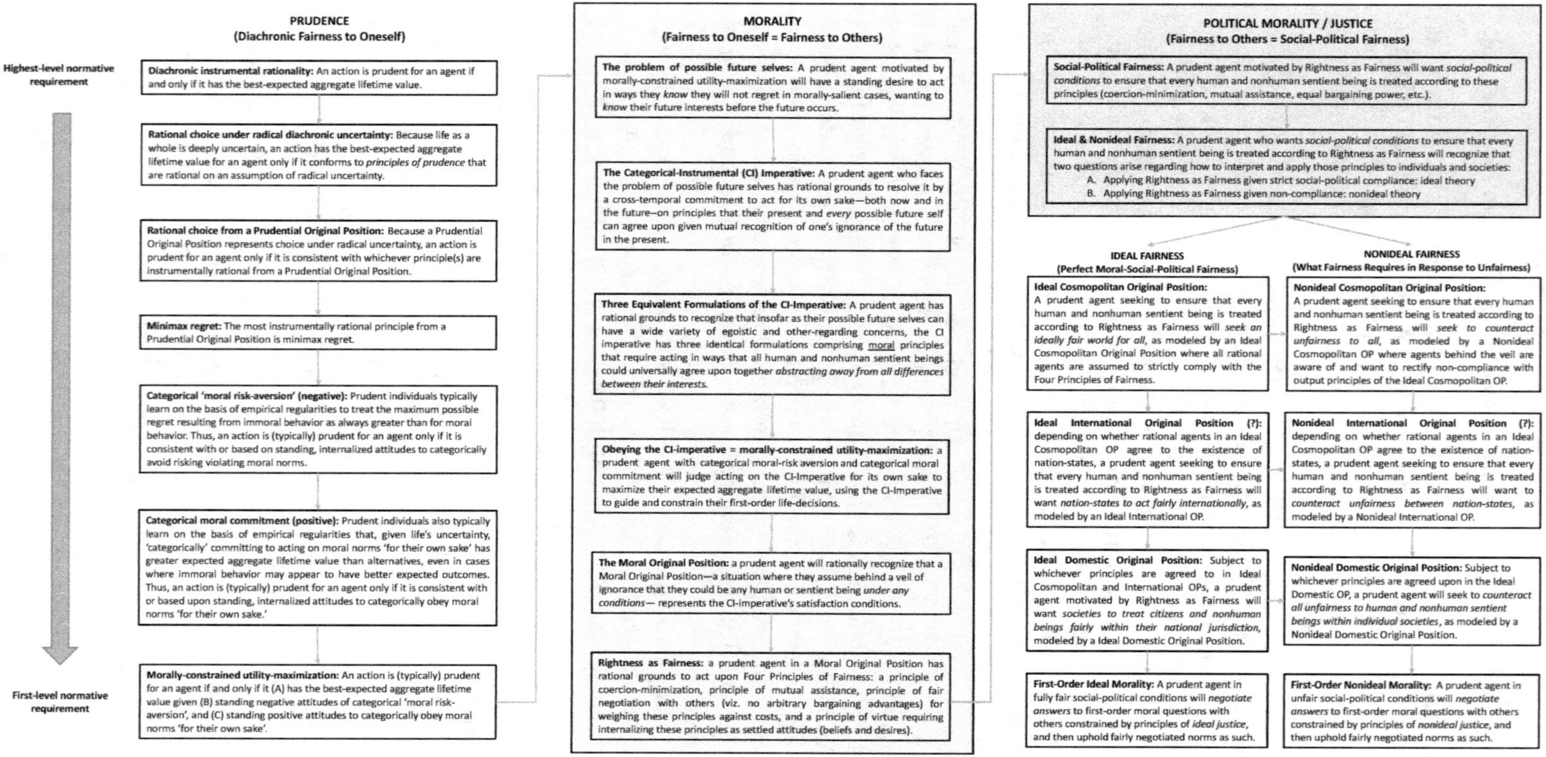

Figure 3.1 Outline of a Unified Normative Theory of Prudence, Morality, and Justice.

morality is indeed the best explanation for a wide variety of relevant phenomena—as Chapter 4 will argue—then the importance of Rawls's original position has been *under*estimated: a variety of iterations of the original position are necessary for understanding the normative nature of prudence, morality, *and* justice (Figure 3.1).

3 A Unified Descriptive Theory of Prudential, Moral, and Social-Political Psychology

Finally, my account entails the following unified descriptive theory of prudential, moral, and social-political psychology (Figure 3.2). Prudent agents learn to worry about the future, wanting to categorically avoid immoral behavior (as too risky) and instead categorically commit themselves to acting morally even if it appears that moral behavior might not maximize personal utility—as prudent agents learn to believe that moral behavior is likely to maximize long-term utility even when it appears it might not. These motivations make it rational for prudent individuals to encounter the 'problem of possible future selves'—that is, to want to know their future interests before the future comes, so that they can avoid possible regret. This leads prudent agents to want to justify their actions to all their possible future selves, but also, in turn, to all possible human and nonhuman sentient beings. This leads prudent agents to (at least implicitly) adopt a Moral Original Position, whereby they ask which principles of action all beings could agree upon from a standpoint of perfect fairness. This in turn leads prudent agents to recognize and aim to conform to Four Principles of Fairness. These Four Principles must then be applied, leading prudent agents to investigate what nonarbitrary bargaining power (viz. the Principle of Fair Negotiation) involves at a social and political level, both at a global level (viz. world affairs) and within particular societies. Because a variety of Social-Political Original Positions represent precisely this, the prudent individual will (at least implicitly) adopt Social-Political Original Positions to arrive at answers to questions of justice, and a Nonideal Original Position to determine what is right and just at a first-order level in an unjust world. Although imperfectly prudent agents (e.g. you, I, and every other human being) may only conform to this psychology imperfectly and perhaps at a very incomplete or implicit level, elements of this descriptive model should show up in the cognition and motivation of people who have internalized prudential motives.

RETROSPECTIVE CONCERNS (PAST)

Memory of regrets for immoral behavior (first, second, and third-personal)

Memory of delayed gratification for moral behavior (first-, second-, and third-personal)

Memory of severe regrets for unfairness
Oneself/others being punished for unfair behavior.
Oneself/others feeling guilty for unfairness.

Memory of delayed gratification for fairness
Oneself and others benefitting long-term by treating others fairly (viz. Four Principles).

Memory of disagreements about how to interpret Four Principles of Fairness

Memory of regrettable social-political unfairness
Recalling disastrous consequences of Nazism, slavery, racism, etc.

Memory of delayed benefits of social-political fairness Better world without Nazism, slavery, racism, etc.

PRUDENTIAL COGNITION

Psychologically internalized normative prudence
- Desire to act in ways w/best expected life-outcomes.
- Profound uncertainty about the future.
- Standing desire to minimize maximum possible regret.
- 'Moral risk-aversion' (See FIGURE 2.5).

HIGH-LEVEL MORAL COGNITION

MORAL ORIGINAL POSITION (implicit or explicit)
Believe & desire to follow Four Principles of Fairness.

Psychologically internalized *moral-prudential conscience*
- Desire to act on Four Principles of Fairness.
- Standing desire to minimize maximum possible regret.

SOCIAL-POLITICAL MORAL COGNITION

Internalized *moral-social-political prudence*
- Desire to act on Four Principles of Fairness.
- Desire to settle Fairness disagreements *non-arbitrarily*.

FIRST-LEVEL MORAL COGNITION

Moral Rightness as Ideal & Nonideal Fairness: interest in conforming to *Four Principles of Fairness* as socially negotiated for ideal and nonideal social-political contexts.

PROSPECTIVE CONCERNS (FUTURE)

Temptation to act immorally

'Moral risk-aversion' (MRA): Wanting to make a (moral) choice one knows one's future self won't regret.

| Categorical unwillingness to risk immoral behavior. | Categorical commitment to morality 'for its own sake'. |

Commitment to the Categorical-Instrumental Imperative (implicit or explicit): act in ways that one's present and every possible future self can mutually accept.

Worry about possible regret from unilateral interpretation of Four Principles of Fairness
'What if what I think is fair coercion or bargaining isn't what other people think? What if they punish me or I feel guilty?'

Cosmopolitan Original Position (Ideal Theory)
Wanting to act according to principles that all persons and nonhuman sentient beings could rationally agree upon behind a veil of ignorance.

| Domestic Original Position (Ideal Theory) | International OP (?) (Ideal Theory) |

Nonideal Original Positions to model what is fair and just in an unjust world - variants for different contexts:
- Global
- International (?)
- Domestic

Figure 3.2 A Unified Descriptive Model of Prudential and Moral Psychology.

4 Conclusion

Some readers will undoubtedly find the theory of morality just defended, based on Chapter 2's findings, to be controversial. However, as we will now see in Chapter 4, it and the theory of prudence it is based upon both cohere with and explain the neurobehavioral phenomena summarized in Chapter 1 better than existing alternatives.

Notes

1 Arvan (2016a): 47–51.
2 Ibid.: 93–7.
3 Ibid.: Chapter 2, §2.4.
4 Ibid.: Chapter 2, §2 and Chapter 3, §5.
5 Ibid.: Chapter 2, §2.
6 For an in-depth discussion of these different types of interests, see Ibid.: Chapter 3, §2 and Chapter 6: §1.3.
7 Ibid.: 90–91, 56–64.
8 An important idea in *Rightness as Fairness* is that agents should not always encounter the problem of possible future selves, the normative problem that makes morality rational. Instead, prudent agents face the problem only when they worry about the future so much that they want to *know* how to act in a way that they will not regret (viz. the prudential psychology defended in Chapter 2 of this book). On my account, rational agents then use the Categorical-Instrumental Imperative to recursively define which other cases they should worry about in a similar fashion, thus delineating the limits of morality from within. Because I argue the Categorical-Instrumental Imperative entails Four Principles of Fairness—one of which is a Principle of Fair Negotiation—this involves socially negotiating fair standards regarding when we should worry about this future in this way, and hence, which of our actions are morally relevant. This is an important result, as one major objection to many ethical theories is that they are too demanding (Wolf 1982, 2012). Rightness as Fairness avoids this charge in that it permits us to socially negotiate how demanding morality is, including when we should or should not engage in moral reasoning.
9 Arvan (2016a): 76, reproduced with permission of Palgrave MacMillan.
10 Dees (2017), Newey (2017): 232.
11 Moore (2017): 526–7, Spencer (2018): 796–7.
12 Spencer (2018): 796.
13 Dees (2017), Moore (2017): 526–7, Newey (2017): 230–1.
14 Batson (2015).
15 See Arvan (2016a): 85–90.
16 Ibid.: 118–27.
17 Bentham [1780]: Chapter 1.
18 *The Family Man* (2000).
19 Augustine [400].
20 Arvan (2016a): 117, reproduced with permission of Palgrave MacMillan.
21 Ibid.: Chapter 4, §2.

22 Ibid.: 117, reproduced with permission of Palgrave MacMillan.
23 Kant [1785]: 4:421.
24 Ibid.: 4:429.
25 Arvan (2012).
26 I do not hold here that all sentient beings can actually rationally agree to things, as nonhuman animals in general do not appear capable of forging agreements. As I argued in Arvan (2016a): 156-57, the interests of sentient nonhuman animals are to be represented *by us* 'by proxy'— by us acting in ways we see would be rational for them to agree to if they possessed capacities for rational agreement.
27 Kant [1785]: 4:433–4.
28 Ibid.: 4:389.
29 Bukoski (2018), Joyce (2007).
30 Arvan (unpublished manuscript).
31 Arvan (2016a): Chapter 1.
32 See Batson (2015): esp. Chapter 4, though May (2018): Chapter 7, §7.3.3–7.4.1 defends the motivational power of moral principles.
33 Compare Korsgaard (2018), Arvan (2016a): Chapters 4–6.
34 Cf. Parfit (2011): Parts 2–5, Darwall (2014), Nebel (2012).
35 See Johnston and Cureton (2018): §9 for an overview. For an argument that Kant's formulas are identical (and hence co-extensive), see Arvan (2012).
36 Rawls (1999a).
37 Rawls (1999b).
38 Rawls (1999a): 475 and §3.
39 Ibid.: 7.
40 Rawls (1993): 297.
41 Rawls (1999a): 4–5, 216–7.
42 Ibid.: 6–10.
43 Farelly (2007), Mills (1997, 2017).
44 See Garner (2012, 2013).
45 Okin (1992).
46 Kuper (2000), Moellendorf (2002).
47 Arvan (2016a): Chapter 5.
48 Jaquet (2017): 318–9.
49 See Baier (1965), Hare (1952), Parfit (2011), and others.
50 Kant [1785]: 4:421.
51 Ibid.: 4:433. Cf. Arvan (2016a): 130, Rawls (1999a): §40.
52 Arvan (2016a): Chapter 6.
53 Newey (2018): 233–4 suggests it is unclear how these are principles of fairness *per se*. Although space constraints prevent protracted discussion, the short answer is that they are properly considered principles of fairness because they are justified by a perfectly fair procedure (the Moral Original Position).
54 Arvan (2016a, 2016b): 6, 153, reproduced with permission of Palgrave MacMillan.
55 Arvan (2016a): 161, 204, 207.
56 See Nozick (1974): Chapters 3 and 5.
57 Singer (1972).
58 Arthur [1981]. Cf. Wenar (2003).

59 Arvan (2016a): 154, reproduced with permission of Palgrave MacMillan.
60 Ibid.: Chapter 4.
61 Ibid.: 7, 154, 176, reproduced with permission of Palgrave MacMillan.
62 Stichter (2018).
63 Compare to Arvan (2016a): 7, 154, 178.
64 Dees (2017), Moore (2017): 526–7, Newey (2017): 230–1.
65 Arvan (2016a): 92–3.
66 Ibid.: 93–109.
67 Dees (2017).
68 See Bukoski (2016, 2017, 2018), Joyce (2007).
69 Post (2008).
70 Dees (2017).
71 Skarlicki and Folger (1997).
72 Nagorski (2012): 138.
73 Dees (2017).
74 Ibid.
75 See Lynch and Palmer (2013).
76 Schmidt (2019).
77 Felson *et al.* (2019).
78 Rosentiel (2008).
79 Fredericks (2019).
80 Dees (2017).
81 Caney (2005), Kuper (2000), Moellendorf (2002).
82 Ibid.
83 Elliot (1984), Garner (2013).
84 Rawls (1999b). Cf. Beitz [1979].
85 Rawls (1993, 1999a).
86 Arvan (2019).
87 Freiman (2017), Gaus (2016), Mills (2005).

References

Arthur, J. [1981]. World Hunger and Moral Obligation: The Case against Singer. In S.M. Cahn (ed.), *Exploring Philosophy: An Introductory Anthology*. Oxford: Oxford University Press. 2009, 142–5.

Arvan, M. (2019). Nonideal Justice as Nonideal Fairness. *Journal of the American Philosophical Association*, 5(2), 208–28.

––––––– (2016a). *Rightness as Fairness: A Moral and Political Theory*. New York: Palgrave MacMillan.

––––––– (2016b). *Errata – Rightness as Fairness: A Moral and Political Theory*, https://philpapers.org/rec/ARVER, retrieved 24 July 2019.

––––––– (2012). Unifying the Categorical Imperative. *Southwest Philosophy Review*, 28(1), 217–25.

––––––– (unpublished manuscript). Reformulating the Categorical Imperative.

Augustine, St. [400]. *The Confessions of St. Augustine*. J.K. Ryan (trans.), New York: Doubleday.

Baier, K. (1965). *The Moral Point of View.* New York: Random House.
Batson, D. (2015). *What's Wrong with Morality? A Social-Psychological Perspective.* Oxford: Oxford University Press.
Beitz, C. [1979]. *Political Theory and International Relations.* Princeton: Princeton University Press, 1999.
Bentham, J. [1780]. *The Collected Works of Jeremy Bentham: An Introduction to the Principles of Morals and Legislation.* Oxford: Clarendon Press, 1996.
Bruckner, D.W. (2003). A Contractarian Account of (Part of) Prudence. *American Philosophical Quarterly, 40*(1), 33–46.
Bukoski, M. (2018). Korsgaard's Arguments for the Value of Humanity. *Philosophical Review, 127*(2), 197–224.
——— (2017). Self-Validation and Internalism in Velleman's Constitutivism. *Philosophical Studies, 174*(11), 2667–86.
——— (2016). A Critique of Smith's Constitutivism. *Ethics, 127*(1), 116–46.
Caney, S. (2005). *Justice Beyond Borders: A Global Political Theory.* Oxford: Oxford University Press.
Darwall, S. (2014). Agreement Matters: Critical Notice of Derek Parfit, On What Matters. *Philosophical Review, 123*(1), 79–105.
Dees, R. (2017). Review of Rightness as Fairness: A Moral and Political Theory. *Notre Dame Philosophical Reviews,* https://ndpr.nd.edu/news/rightness-as-fairness-a-moral-and-political-theory/, retrieved 5 June 2019.
Elliot, R. (1984). Rawlsian Justice and non-Human Animals. *Journal of Applied Philosophy, 1*(1), 95–106.
Farelly, C. (2007). Justice in Ideal Theory: A Refutation. *Political Studies, 55*(4), 844–64.
Felson, J., Adamczyk, A., & Thomas, C. (2019). How and Why Have Attitudes about Cannabis Legalization Changed So Much? *Social Science Research, 78,* 12–27.
Fredericks, B. (2019). Poll Shows 'Dramatic Shift' in Americans' Attitude Toward Abortion. *New York Post.* https://nypost.com/2019/02/25/poll-shows-dramatic-shift-in-americans-attitude-toward-abortion/, retrieved 15 July 2019.
Freiman, C. (2017). *Unequivocal Justice.* New York: Routledge.
Garner, R. (2013). *A Theory of Justice for Animals: Animal Rights in a Nonideal World.* Oxford: Oxford University Press.
——— (2012). Rawls, Animals and Justice: New Literature, Same Response. *Res Publica, 18*(2), 159–72.
Gaus, G. (2016). *The Tyranny of the Ideal: Justice in a Diverse Society.* Princeton: Princeton University Press.
Hare, R.M. (1952). *The Language of Morals.* Oxford: Clarendon Press.
Jaquet, F. (2018). Marcus Arvan, Rightness as Fairness: A Moral and Political Theory. *Dialectica, 72*(2), 315–20.
Johnson, R. & Cureton, A. (2018). Kant's Moral Philosophy. *The Stanford Encyclopedia of Philosophy,* E.N. Zalta (ed.), https://plato.stanford.edu/archives/spr2018/entries/kant-moral/.

Joyce, R. (2007). *The Myth of Morality*. Cambridge, UK: Cambridge University Press.
Kant, I. [1788]. *Critique of Practical Reason*, In M.J. Gregor (ed.), *The Cambridge Edition of the Works of Immanuel Kant: Practical Philosophy*. Cambridge: Cambridge University Press, 1996, 133–271.
——— [1785]. *Groundwork of the Metaphysics of Morals*, in Ibid., 38–108.
Korsgaard, C.M. (2018). *Fellow Creatures: Our Obligations to Other Animals*. Oxford: Oxford University Press.
Kuper, A. (2000). Rawlsian Global Justice: Beyond the Law of Peoples to a Cosmopolitan Law of Persons. *Political Theory*, 28(5), 640–74.
Lynch, S.N. & Palmer, K. (2013). Republican Senator with Gay Son now Backs Gay Marriage. *Reuters*. https://www.reuters.com/article/us-usa-portman-gaymarriage/republican-senator-with-gay-son-now-backs-gay-marriage-idUSBRE92E0G020130315, retrieved 2 July 2019.
May, J. (2018). *Regard for Reason in the Moral Mind*. Oxford: Oxford University Press.
Mills, C. (2017). *Black Rights / White Wrongs: The Critique of Racial Liberalism*. Oxford: Oxford University Press.
——— (2005). "Ideal Theory" as Ideology. *Hypatia*, 20(3), 165–84.
——— (1997). *The Racial Contract*. Ithaca: Cornell University Press.
Moellendorf, D. (2002). *Cosmopolitan Justice*. Oxford: Oxford University Press.
Moore, L. (2017). A Critical Review of Rightness as Fairness: A Moral and Political Theory. *Res Publica*, 23(4), 523–9.
Nagorski, A. (2012). *Hitlerland: American Eyewitnesses to the Nazi Rise to Power*. New York: Simon & Schuster.
Nebel, J. (2012). A Counterexample to Parfit's Rule Consequentialism. *Journal of Ethics and Social Philosophy*, 6(2), 1–10.
Newey, C.A. (2017). Marcus Arvan, Rightness as Fairness: A Moral and Political Theory. *Ethics*, 128(1), 230–5.
Nozick, R. (1974). *Anarchy, State, and Utopia*. New York: Basic Books.
Okin, S.M. (1991). Justice, Gender, and the Family. *Philosophy and Public Affairs*, 20(1), 77–97.
Parfit, D. (2011). *On What Matters, Vols. 1&2*. Oxford: Oxford University Press.
Post, S.G. [Ed.] (2008). *Altruism and Health: Perspectives from Empirical Research*. Oxford: Oxford University Press.
Pronin, E., Olivola, C.Y., & Kennedy, K.A. (2008). Doing Unto Future Selves as You Would Do Unto Others: Psychological Distance and Decision Making. *Personality and Social Psychology Bulletin*, 34(2), 224–36.
Rawls, J. (1999a). *A Theory of Justice: Revised Edition*. Cambridge, MA: The Belknap Press of Harvard University Press.
——— (1999b). *The Law of Peoples, with 'The Idea of Public Reason Revisited'*. Cambridge, MA: Harvard University Press.
——— (1993). *Political Liberalism*. New York: Columbia University Press.

Rosentiel, T. (2008). Public Attitudes toward the War in Iraq: 2003–2008. *Pew Research Center.* https://www.pewresearch.org/2008/03/19/public-attitudes-toward-the-war-in-iraq-20032008/, retrieved 15 July 2019.

Schmidt, S. (2019). Americans' Views Flipped on Gay Rights. How Did Minds Change So Quickly? *The Washington Post.* https://www.washingtonpost.com/local/social-issues/americans-views-flipped-on-gay-rights-how-did-minds-change-so-quickly/2019/06/07/ae256016-8720-11e9-98c1-e945ae5db8fb_story.html?noredirect=on&utm_term=.91629d24a229, retrieved 2 July 2019.

Singer, P. (1972). Famine, Affluence, and Morality, *Philosophy and Public Affairs*, *1*(3), 229–43.

Skarlicki, D.P. & Folger, R. (1997). Retaliation in the Workplace: The Roles of Distributive, Procedural, and Interactional Justice. *Journal of Applied Psychology*, *82*(3), 434–44.

Spencer, E. (2018). Rightness as Fairness: A Moral and Political Theory, Written by Marcus Arvan. *Journal of Moral Philosophy*, *15*(6), 795–8.

Stichter, M. (2018). *Ethical Expertise and Virtuous Skills.* Cambridge: Cambridge University Press.

The Family Man (2000). https://www.imdb.com/title/tt0218967/, retrieved 5 June 2019.

Wenar, L. (2003). What We Owe to Distant Others. *Politics, Philosophy and Economics*, *2*(3), 283–304.

Wolf, S. (2012). 'One Thought Too Many': Love, Morality, and the Ordering of Luck, Value, and Commitment. In U. Heuer & G. Lang (eds.), *Themes from the Ethics of Bernard Williams.* Oxford: Oxford University Press, 71–94.

——— (1982). Moral Saints. *Journal of Philosophy*, *79*(8), 419–39.

4 A Unified Neurofunctional Theory of Prudence and Morality?

Chapter 1 provided an overview of the emerging behavioral neuroscience of prudence and morality. Chapters 2 and 3 then outlined a unified normative and descriptive philosophical theory of prudence and morality—a theory of diachronic reasoning that I will now call *Prudence and Morality as Fairness to Oneself and Others*. This chapter argues that this theory is the most compelling current explanation of the behavioral neuroscience in two respects: (1) as a normative explanation of why various capacities, dispositions, and brain regions should be involved in prudential and moral cognition, and (2) as a descriptive explanation of how those capacities actually function in prudential and moral psychology. A complete examination of behavioral neuroscience would require a more expansive examination than this chapter or book can provide. This chapter's aim instead is to outline why this book's theory explains a variety of behavioral-neuroscientific findings better than alternatives, and thus warrants further empirical and philosophical attention in future research.

1 Two Types of Explanations: Normative and Descriptive

There are many different philosophical theories of the nature of explanation. For example, theories of scientific explanation include the Deductive-Nomological (DN), Statistically Relevant (SR), Causal Mechanical, Unificationist, and Pragmatic models.[1] There are analogous debates about the nature of metaphysical explanation,[2] moral explanation,[3] and normative explanation.[4] We cannot settle these debates here. Instead, this chapter works with an intuitive understanding of what it is for a theory to explain target phenomena, as any adequate philosophical theory of explanation should plausibly cohere with pre-theoretic judgments about what constitutes an explanation.[5] The chapter will then use seven principles of theory selection adapted from the philosophy of science to evaluate how well this book's theory explains Chapter 1's behavioral neuroscience compared to alternatives.

To begin, consider paradigmatic cases of explanation in everyday life—for example, explanations of evidence in a courtroom. Suppose a defendant is on trial for murder. Their fingerprints were found at the scene of the crime, several eyewitnesses reported observing the defendant commit the murder, web searches related to murder were found on their computer in the days leading up to the crime, and their cell phone Global Positioning System (GPS) indicates that they were at the murder scene during the crime. The prosecuting attorney argues that the best explanation of this evidence is that the defendant is guilty. The defense attorney then offers an alternative theory: that the defendant is an innocent victim of a massive conspiracy to frame them for the crime. Which explanation of the evidence is better? Assuming the defense attorney provides no clear evidence for the existence of a conspiracy, the jury will likely arrive at the conclusion that the prosecuting attorney's explanation is more plausible. Among other things, the prosecutor's theory is a simpler, less *ad hoc* explanation of the evidence.

Bearing this example in mind, we can see that this book's theory may explain the behavioral neuroscience summarized in Chapter 1 in two distinct ways. This book's theory is both normative and descriptive. First, it provides a normative theory of how people should reason, the motivations and emotional responses they should develop, and how they should act in order to act in normatively prudent and moral ways. Second, the theory provides a descriptive psychological theory of how people who are normatively prudent and moral actually do reason, the motivations they have, and how they act. Consequently, the theory simultaneously encompasses two different types of explanations.

First, the theory comprises a normative teleofunctional explanation of why various capacities and brain regions *should* be involved in prudential and moral cognition. Teleofunctionalism is the view that mental-states should be individuated by what they are for—that is, by their 'proper-function'.[6] Although teleofunctionalists normally understand proper-functions in descriptive causal terms (including evolutionary terms), this book's theory holds that particular capacities (such as mental time-travel) serve particular normative functions: the function of generating normatively prudent and moral behavior. Consequently, this book's theory constitutes a normative explanation for why science should find particular brain regions, capacities, and behavioral dispositions to be involved in prudential and moral cognition, playing particular functions.

This kind of explanation is important for the following reason. As we saw in Chapter 1, empirical findings naturally raise normative explanatory questions. For example, why should we expect to find moral judgment (i.e. moral beliefs) to involve the *precuneus*, a part of the brain associated with episodic memories of events affecting oneself? Similarly, why should we expect to find moral judgment to involve the *angular gyrus*, an area associated with representing the mental states of individuals in cartoons and stories? This book's theory entails answers to these questions, explaining why prudential and moral cognition should involve these and other brain regions and their associated functions.

Second, this book's theory constitutes a descriptive neurofunctional explanation of how various cognitive functions actually function when generating normatively prudent and moral behavior. This kind of explanation is important as well. For in addition to a normative explanation of which brain regions, capacities, and processes should be involved in prudential and moral cognition, we also have grounds to desire an empirically adequate theory of how they actually do function to generate normatively prudent and moral behavior.

Consequently, although this book cannot resolve complex questions about the nature of explanation, we may be able to judge—at least preliminarily, utilizing well-known principles of theory selection—whether this book's theory is presently the most compelling explanation of Chapter 1's behavioral neuroscience in both respects: normatively and descriptively. Finally, we will also see that as a descriptive explanation of prudential and moral cognition, the theory makes novel predictions we may use to confirm or disconfirm the theory in future empirical work.

2 Explanations and Underdetermination of Theory by Evidence

In order to evaluate this book's theory and compare it to alternatives, we must discuss another famous issue in the philosophy of science: the problem of underdetermination of theory by evidence.[7] In brief, this problem is that at any given point in time, a large (and potentially infinite) number of theories will be consistent with the same empirical evidence. Consider two theories of planetary motion: the modern Copernican theory that the Earth and other planets revolve around the Sun, and the ancient Ptolemaic theory that the Earth is stationary and the Sun and other planets revolve around the Earth. Some readers might understandably think that Copernicus' theory has been confirmed by and Ptolemaic astronomy refuted by empirical observation. However, as Stephen Hawking and Leonard Mlodinow note, this is incorrect: Ptolemaic astronomy is in principle consistent with all of our empirical evidence.[8] This is because of the *Quine-Duhem thesis*, which holds that no hypothesis can be tested in isolation, but rather only relative to background assumptions.[9] Allow me to explain.

Prior to Copernican theory, Ptolemaic theorists faced a problem: their theory held that all astronomical objects orbit the Earth in circles. However, observations seemed to contradict this hypothesis, as planets were observed to display 'retrograde motion'—appearing to move forward in their orbit, then backwards, and then forward again—which Ptolemaic theory did not predict.[10] Did these observations disconfirm the theory? No. For all Ptolemaic theorists had to do in order to render the theory consistent with the new evidence was *alter* the theory's background assumptions. They did this by introducing 'epicycles', positing that heavenly bodies orbit in smaller circular orbits around their main orbits. The resulting version of Ptolemaic astronomy is consistent with retrograde motion. Further, the Ptolemaic hypothesis that the Earth is stationary can also be rendered consistent with all empirical observations though the present. This is because Einstein's theory of relativity (which has made a wide variety of accurate predictions) entails that there is no such thing as absolute motion. According to General Relativity's equivalence principle, it is impossible to ascertain by experiment whether an object is stationary in a gravitational field or accelerating in motion: the two are observationally equivalent.[11] Whether an object appears to be moving depends upon the *reference frame* one adopts in observation: it is equally correct to say that from the standpoint of observations on Earth, the Earth is stationary and all heavenly bodies revolve around it, but from the reference frame of the Sun, the Sun is stationary and all things revolve around *it*. Consequently, Ptolemaic astronomy has never been observationally disconfirmed: the theory can be made consistent with our empirical evidence by altering its background assumptions.

The point of the Quine-Duhem thesis is that this phenomenon is true of theories in general. As another example, consider Young Earth Creationism, the theory that the Universe is only several thousand years old. Although it is tempting to believe that empirical observations disconfirm this theory, Young Earth Creationism's background assumptions can be revised to 'explain' all observed evidence. For example, Young Earth Creationists can claim that God put fossils into the ground several-thousand years ago, made fossils' radioactive properties appear to indicate that the Universe is 13.8 billion years old, and so on. In this way, we can see how a variety of competing theories can be rendered consistent with the same empirical evidence.

However, there is an important qualification here. Although multiple theories can be made consistent with any body of evidence, not all theories seem to explain the evidence equally well. Ptolemaic astronomy and Young Earth Creationism are widely rejected today. Why? Although we cannot resolve debates about the nature of explanation here, the dominant view in the philosophy of science is that metaphilosophical principles of theory selection should be used to determine which theory is the best explanation of the available evidence.[12] For example, although Ptolemaic astronomy can be rendered consistent with our empirical evidence, the Copernican model provides a much simpler and more unified explanation—one that does not involve arbitrarily introducing epicycles to explain retrograde motion. This, in brief, is why the Copernican theory is widely accepted and Ptolematic theory rejected. Copernican theory provides a simpler and more unified explanation of observed phenomena.

There is ongoing debate about which principles of theory selection we should use to evaluate theories.[13] Because we cannot settle these issues, I want to assume the Seven Principles of Theory Selection that I defended in *Rightness as Fairness*—principles that I argued are plausible and routinely appealed to in scientific practice:

Seven Principles of Theory Selection
1 *Firm Foundations*: theories based on common human observation—or observations that are taken to be obvious, incontrovertible fact by all or almost all observers—should be preferred over theories based on controversial observations that may seem true to some investigators but not to others.
2 *Internal Coherence:* all things being equal, and subject to Firm Foundations, theories with fewer or no internal contradictions should be preferred over theories with more.
3 *External Coherence*: all things being equal, and subject to Firm Foundations, theories cohering with more known facts and observations should be preferred over theories cohering with fewer.

4 *Explanatory Power*: all things being equal, and subject to Firm Foundations, theories explaining more facts and observations should be preferred over theories explaining fewer.
5 *Unity*: all things being equal, and subject to Firm Foundations, theories unifying disparate phenomena, showing how they have a common explanation, should be preferred over theories providing more fragmentary explanations.
6 *Parsimony*: all things being equal, and subject to Firm Foundations, theories that successfully explain phenomena with fewer facts or entities should be preferred over theories explaining the same phenomena with more.
7 *Fruitfulness*: all things being equal, and subject to Firm Foundations, theories solving more existing theoretical or practical problems should be preferred over theories solving fewer.[14]

Assuming these principles are correct—and I will attempt to make their meaning precise enough for our purposes in discussion below—let us compare this book's theory to alternative normative and descriptive explanations of Chapter 1's behavioral neuroscience.

3 Comparing Current Explanations of the Behavioral Neuroscience

Two different kinds of theories might explain Chapter 1's behavioral neuroscience. First, there are normative ethical theories— theories of what morality normatively requires. Such theories provide normative explanations of how moral cognition *should* work when people behave morally. For example, Aristotelian virtue ethics entails that people who act as they morally ought to should act from settled virtues of character. Similarly, Kantian ethics implies that people who act morally should (at least implicitly) cognize the Categorical Imperative, representing and acting on universalizable maxims that respect the humanity of themselves and others. Second, there are purely descriptive theories of moral psychology, which purport to explain moral cognition without necessarily taking a stance on normative matters. I will now use the principles of theory selection discussed above to argue that this book's theory is a better normative and descriptive explanation of Chapter 1's behavioral neuroscience than various normative and descriptive alternatives.

3.1 The Theory Presented: A Strong Normative and Descriptive Explanation

In Chapter 1, we saw that prudential and moral cognition involve all of the following:

i **Mental time-travel:** the capacity to simulate the past and future.
ii **Other-perspective-taking (OPT):** simulating other beings' perspectives.
iii **Risk-aversion:** preferring less desirable but more certain outcomes, including 'moral risk-aversion', which involves '[erring] on the side of caution to avoid imposing intolerable costs on others'.[15]

This book's theory provides strong explanations for all three findings. First, it normatively explains why prudential and moral cognition should involve all three phenomena (Figure 3.1). Chapter 2 argued that normatively prudent agents typically internalize a very specific form of 'moral risk-aversion' based on past-experience throughout childhood, adolescence, and adulthood. We then saw in Chapter 3 that this form of moral risk-aversion makes it rational to engage in forward-directed mental time-travel involving the problem of possible future selves, where the agent worries about their possible future selves, wanting to know which self they will be so that they can make a decision they will not regret. Finally, we saw in Chapter 3 that normatively rational agents solve the problem of possible future selves by acting on the Categorical-Instrumental Imperative, a principle that requires imagining and caring about the perspectives of other human and nonhuman sentient beings (viz. the Moral Original Position). The theory thus normatively explains why we should find mental time-travel, OPT, and risk-aversion implicated in prudential and moral cognition. Second, the theory provides a descriptive explanation—a neurofunctional model—of how these three capacities actually function and interact to generate normatively prudent and moral behavior (Figure 3.2).

The theory also normatively and descriptively explains a variety of other behavioral neuroscientific findings. In Chapter 1, we saw that twelve regions of the brain's *Default Mode Network* (DMN) are implicated in moral judgment (i.e. moral belief) across a wide variety of tasks. This book's theory normatively explains why behavioral neuroscience should find those regions to be involved in moral belief, while also providing a detailed descriptive explanation of how various DMN regions and capacities actually interact to generate moral belief. First, this book's theory holds that our moral beliefs are ultimately rooted in prudential uncertainty about the future (viz. the 'problem of possible selves'). On the account defended, the motivations that give rise to this uncertainty (wanting to act in ways one's possible future selves will not regret) are rooted in turn in our memory of past moral-prudential mistakes: cases where—as children, adolescents, or adults—we were 'too certain' about the future, thinking we could benefit from immoral behavior only to suffer punishment or guilt instead. Further, on the present theory's account, the kinds of imprudent 'moral risk-taking' that children and adolescents often engage in is progressively extinguished through social punishment and internalized feelings of guilt and regret, which prudent agents recall through episodic memory and want to avoid in their future behavior. This book's theory thus normatively explains why two particular DMN regions—the *vmPFC* and *precuneus*, which involve episodic memory, risk, uncertainty, concern for the future, and extinction of unrewarded behavior—should be involved in moral belief, and descriptively how they are involved.

Second, the theory normatively explains why (i) a person's sense of self, (ii) concern for their own future selves, and (iii) desire to adopt other beings' perspectives should all be concurrently involved in moral belief—and indeed, why concern for one's possible future selves and for others should have bidirectional causal influence. This is because, on my account, prudentially rational concern for oneself in the present and future (viz. 'the problem of possible future selves') makes it rational to care about the possible effects one's actions have on others, *vis-à-vis* the Categorical-Instrumental Imperative: the principle theorized to underlie our moral beliefs (about coercion, mutual-benefit, fair bargaining, and virtue). This book's theory thus explains why eight DMN regions involved in the representation of oneself, one's future selves, and others' perspectives—the *dmPFC, TPJ, MTG, STC, MOG, TP, FG, ITG* (which are associated with sense of self, concern for future selves, and representing others' perspectives)—should all be involved in moral belief. Further, this book's theory explains why stimulating and inhibiting future-concern and concern for others should have demonstrated bidirectional causal effects on prudential and moral behavior.[16] The theory also provides a detailed descriptive explanation of how capacities associated with these brain regions interact to generate normatively prudent and moral behavior (see Figure 3.2).

A Unified Neurofunctional Theory? 103

Third, this book's theory normatively and descriptively explains why and how the two remaining DMN regions—*Wernicke's area* and the *angular gyrus*—are involved in moral belief. First, the theory normatively predicts that *Wernicke's area* should be involved in moral belief, as inner monologue plays a central role in the theory, both in episodic memory (viz. 'I regretted lying before. I should not lie this time') and prospectively (viz. 'I wish I knew the right thing to do, so I won't regret what I do'). Second, the theory normatively explains why and how the *angular gyrus*, the neural region associated with understanding stories, is involved in moral belief, as on the theory defended, moral and prudential learning both involve learning from and recalling stories—including stories from one's own past, stories from others, fictional tragedies, redemption stories, and so on (see Figure 3.2).

Finally, the theory explains why the five additional DMN regions reported in Chapter 1—the *cingulate gyrus, orbitofrontal cortex* (OFC), *amygdala, cuneus,* and *lingual gyrus*—should be implicated in and function in moral sensitivity (i.e. monitoring and recognizing morally salient details of a given situation, including value conflicts, in ways that involve empathy). First, the theory holds that normatively prudent, moral individuals monitor and recognize whether a situation is morally relevant—and if so, how several different and potentially conflicting values apply—through concern for cross-temporal contingencies, a capacity associated with the OFC. This is because, on my theory, moral concern emerges out of concern for one's future self (viz. the problem of possible future selves), and the Categorical-Instrumental Imperative is used to recursively determine whether a situation is morally relevant, and if so, how different conflicting values apply (viz. Four Principles of Fairness). Second, the kind of concern for cross-temporal contingencies that the theory holds underlies prudent and moral cognition, 'moral risk-aversion', involves the suppression of willingness to gamble on outcomes—a capacity associated with both the OFC and *cuneus*. Third, the theory holds that we develop and maintain this form of moral risk-aversion through fear conditioning, memory of past moral-prudential errors, and positive reinforcement—capacities associated with the *cingulate gyrus, lingual gyrus,* and *amygdala*. Fourth, the theory holds that the problem of possible future selves makes it rational to be concerned with all of the ways one's actions in the present could possibly affect one's future selves, and by extension, all of the counterfactual ways one's actions might affect the interests of other human and nonhuman sentient beings—capacities associated with the OFC. Fifth, the theory explains why (in morally salient cases) several specific emotions associated with the *amygdala* should be involved in moral sensitivity: namely, fear, anxiety, sadness, and anger. Specifically, on the theory defended, the prudential underpinning of moral sensitivity is possible immense regret for immoral behavior, which prudent individuals typically learn they should fear and have anxiety about, and which can also involve intense retrospective anger and sadness at oneself for 'taking dumb risks' in the past. Sixth, the theory explains specifically why and how the *lingual gyrus* should be involved in moral sensitivity, as visual memories of the negative consequences of past moral-violations (e.g. others' expressions of anger or hurt) are a particularly vivid way of recalling why the agent should not risk immoral behavior. Seventh, the theory explains precisely why psychopaths demonstrate poor prudential and moral performance due to specific deficits associated with the above DMN areas, as psychopaths have deficits in capacities to learn from fear-conditioning,[17] vividly imagine the future,[18] experience empathy in OPT,[19] and use prospective regret to inhibit risky, unethical behavior.[20]

Finally, the theory also normatively and descriptively explains a variety of other empirical findings not discussed in Chapter 1. First, it explains the finding that in moral development, moral belief and sensitivity do indeed appear to emerge out of instrumental concern. Children appear to initially learn moral behavior instrumentally—primarily caring about social reward and punishment—only internalizing this punishment-reward system in their own psychology (through guilt and remorse) much later, after a great deal of conditioning and socialization. This is precisely what this book's developmental theory holds (see Figures 2.1–2.5).[21] Second, the theory explains empirical findings that adults also often appear to reason instrumentally about moral issues[22] (e.g. tending to cheat when it appears to have greater benefits than not[23]), while also explaining findings that certain people have moral integrity vis-à-vis internalized dispositions to obey moral principles for their own sake.[24] Third, as we will see in more detail in Chapter 5, the theory even predicts 'Hubris syndrome', an empirical phenomenon in which people in positions of power demonstrate compromised dispositions to simulate and care about other people's perspectives and interests, and compromised dispositions to obey moral norms, *because* they are less risk-averse.[25] Fourth, the theory predicts and explains why people tend to engage in 'mediocre' or 'B+' moral behavior—that is, behavior that is not extremely altruistic, but instead coheres with norms that others typically follow.[26] For as we have already seen, the theory normatively predicts that it is rational to act on principles that constitute a compromise between self-interest and altruism. Finally, the theory also coheres normatively and descriptively with a wide variety of findings, including the finding that moral forms of OPT *are* neurofunctionally related to imaginatively simulating one's possible future selves, as the theory holds this is how moral individuals *should and do* cognize morality (see Figures 3.1 and 3.2).[27]

Consequently, this book's theory appears to satisfy all Seven Principles of Theory Selection mentioned earlier to a high degree. First, the theory has comparatively Firm Foundations. On the one hand, it is based upon intuitively plausible observations of how normatively prudent and moral people tend to think, feel, and act (see Chapters 2 and 3, as well as Figures 2.1–2.5, 3.1, and 3.2). Further, we have just seen that the theory coheres with and explains a multitude of empirical findings in behavioral neuroscience. Second, the theory has high Internal Coherence, as it normatively and descriptively explains both prudence and morality in an internally consistent manner. Third, the theory has high External Coherence. As we just saw above, the theory normatively predicts why a wide variety of brain regions and capacities empirically implicated in prudential and moral cognition should be involved in both types of cognition. To be sure, many of the brain regions mentioned above are involved in other areas of cognition, not just prudential and moral cognition.[28] The relevant point for our purposes is simply that this book's theory normatively predicts that all of the brain regions and capacities that science has found to be implicated in prudential and moral cognition *should* be involved in moral cognition—something we will see other theories do not normatively predict to a comparable extent. The theory also coheres with many plausible normative claims about prudence (see Chapter 2), as well as prominent normative claims about morality (accounting for common deontological, consequentialist, contractualist, and virtue ethical insights—see Chapter 3). Fourth, the theory has high normative and descriptive Explanatory Power. The theory provides a single normative and descriptive explanation of prudence, morality, and political morality, reducing morality—both descriptively and normatively—to prudence (see Figures 3.1 and 3.2). Fifth, the theory has a maximally high level of normative and descriptive Unity: it normatively reduces prudence, morality, and political morality to instrumental rationality (Figure 3.2), and descriptively reduces prudential and moral cognition to a unified process of instrumental deliberation, risk-aversion, mental-time-travel, and OPT (Figure 3.1). Sixth, the theory is Parsimonious: it normatively and descriptively reduces prudence and morality to behavioral neuroscientific phenomena combined with our simple instrumental concept of rationality. Finally, the theory has a high level of Fruitfulness. First, it promises compelling resolutions to various normative philosophical problems. As we saw in Chapter 3, Rightness as Fairness plausibly unifies competing moral frameworks (deontology, consequentialism, contractualism, and virtue ethics). It also provides an explanation of how political morality (i.e. social and political justice) relates to morality and prudence (viz. Social-Political Original Positions necessary for applying Rightness as Fairness to social-political contexts). The theory also makes a variety of potentially fruitful empirical predictions. It predicts that prudent individuals tempted to behave immorally should avoid immoral behavior by virtue of wanting to avoid decisions they might regret (viz. the 'problem of possible future selves'), and by identifying actions they will not regret with moral actions pursued for their own sake. It also provides a testable developmental model of how children, adolescents, and adults learn to become prudent and internalize moral dispositions. Finally, it provides a general neurofunctional theory of what prudential and moral cognition consist in (Figure 3.2). The theory's predictions can thus serve as the basis for hypotheses for future research to investigate in order to determine how empirically accurate—either in whole or in part—the theory is.

3.2 Explanatory Advantages over Alternative Normative Moral Theories

What about other normative ethical theories? How well do they normatively and descriptively explain the existing evidence from behavioral neuroscience? Although we cannot examine every normative ethical theory, a survey of five leading moral frameworks should suffice to outline how this book's theory compares to alternatives.

3.2.1 Advantages over Aristotelian Virtue Ethics

Aristotelian virtue ethics holds that morality is a matter of developing and acting upon moral virtues, which are understood as standing dispositions to think, feel, and act in ways that are beneficial (both for the agent and others) over a complete life.[29] According to Aristotelians, moral virtues—traits like honesty, courage, kindness, and so on—are learned through habituation (i.e. repetitive practice). Further, at least at some level, the rationality of the

A Unified Neurofunctional Theory? 107

virtues becomes understood by the virtuous agent: they come to understand how the virtues are beneficial to themselves and to others over the course of life as a whole.

Because Aristotelianism holds that virtuous agents understand that the virtues are beneficial over a complete life, it might be argued that Aristotelianism normatively predicts that mental time-travel (and hence the *TPJ*) should be involved in moral belief and motivation: specifically, that a normatively prudent and moral agent should imagine their life as a whole when developing or acting upon the virtues. It might also be argued that insofar as Aristotelian virtue ethics holds that virtues are learned and lost by habitual practice—practices that are typically socially incentivized (by the punishment of dishonest behavior, etc.)—Aristotelianism normatively predicts that moral belief and motivation will involve episodic and long-term memory, fear conditioning, and so on (viz. the *amygdala*). Finally, it could be argued that virtues in some way or other involve risk-aversion, simulating other people's perspectives (OPT), and so on.

However, there are several problems here. First, Aristotelian virtue ethicists have never explicitly made any such predictions given the normative resources of their theoretical framework. For example, although Aristotelians argue that honesty is a virtue learned through habit, I am unaware of any Aristotelian who argues that moral beliefs in general—including beliefs about honesty—involve mental time-travel, OPT, risk-aversion, or internal monologue, all of which are capacities associated with DMN regions that have been repeatedly implicated in moral beliefs across various tasks. Given that Aristotelian virtue theories have never directly predicted these phenomena, Aristotelianism can at most be 'retrofitted' to explain the above findings in much the same way that Ptolemaic astronomy can be adapted to observations of retrograde planetary motion.

Second, the claim that Aristotelianism predicts that agents should imaginatively simulate the past and future in moral decision-making in general (as the empirical science indicates) sits poorly with the standard Aristotelian thesis that once virtues are internalized as a matter of habit, the virtuous agent will act from those settled dispositions for their own sake. Indeed, without some further normative analysis of why virtues in general should involve imaginatively simulating the past and future—such as the kind of account this book's theory provides—the claim that Aristotelianism predicts that mental time-travel should be involved in moral cognition across a wide variety of phenomena (as science has found) is both *ad hoc* and *post hoc*.

Third, some neurobehavioral findings are in tension with Aristotelian virtue ethics. For example, Aristotelianism holds that virtues are excellences of character. However, as we have seen, empirical data indicates that most people's actual moral behavior is decidedly 'mediocre'. Although it is open to Aristotelians to argue (as they often have[30]) that this merely shows that moral virtues are rare, this book's theory explains the data more straightforwardly, holding that 'mediocre' moral behavior (viz. fair compromise between self-interest and the interests of others) is rational, thus explaining why most people only engage in 'B+'-level moral behavior. Second, Aristotelianism provides no normative or descriptive explanation for Hubris syndrome: for why individuals in positions of power should show compromised dispositions to imagine or care other people's perspectives. Because Aristotelianism holds that virtues are settled psychological dispositions, Aristotelianism suggests that virtuous people should still behave virtuously in positions of power. Conversely, this book's theory holds that the rationality of morality (viz. Rightness as Fairness) is rooted in prudential 'moral risk-aversion'—allowing, as we will see in Chapter 5, that moral risk-aversion may be less rational (or even irrational) for people in positions of great power. Although this is a disturbing result, empirical research on Hubris Syndrome coheres with this analysis better than with Aristotelianism.

For these reasons, this book's theory appears to be a more compelling normative and descriptive explanation than Aristotelianism of the behavioral neuroscience summarized in Chapter 1.

3.2.2 Advantages over Utilitarianism

Utilitarianism can also be adapted to cohere with Chapter 1's behavioral neuroscience, at least in part. For example, it is possible for utilitarians to argue that moral belief and sensitivity involve risk-aversion, as Mill argued that utility is generally maximized by conforming to secondary social moral rules (e.g. 'Don't tell lies!') even if the personal benefits of immorality might appear to be greater.[31] Utilitarianism can also be argued to cohere with the idea that morality involves mental time-travel and OPT, as both phenomena seem vital to appreciating the social consequences of one's actions. Nevertheless, Utilitarianism appears to offer less compelling normative explanations for a number of other findings, and an unsatisfactory descriptive explanation of how human moral psychology actually functions.

First, Utilitarianism clashes with the observation that people tend to engage in 'B+'-level moral behavior. According to utilitarians, morality normatively requires us to maximize social utility, which many argue makes utilitarianism very demanding.[32] For example, Peter Singer uses utilitarian grounds to argue that morality requires individuals to give up most of their luxuries to address world poverty.[33] However, people tend to be far more self-interested than this.[34] Utilitarians explain this tension in several ways. Singer emphasizes that Utilitarianism is merely a normative theory of how people ought to behave, not a descriptive theory of how they actually do behave.[35] Others argue that Utilitarianism is not as demanding as it may appear.[36] Although these are possible explanations, this book's theory provides a normatively and descriptively more parsimonious, unified, and (predictively) powerful explanation. It holds that normatively prudent and moral agents have rational grounds not to be extremely altruistic, but instead approximate compromises between self-interest and the interests of others via social negotiation. And indeed, this is more or less what the behavioral neuroscience finds: that people engage in only moderately other-regarding behavior, tailoring their behavior to socially recognized norms.[37] This book's theory thus appears to be a better explanation of the neuroscience than utilitarianism. It provides a simpler, more unified descriptive explanation of why people actually tend to behave in the 'mediocre' ways that they do and normative explanation of why they should act that way (viz. fair compromise between selfishness and altruism, rather than the extreme impartiality utilitarianism requires).

3.2.3 Advantages over Kantianism

Kantianism also appears to cohere poorly with the aforementioned neuroscience. On the one hand, it may be possible to adapt Kantianism to some empirical findings. For example, Kantians could argue that acting according to the Categorical Imperative requires risk-aversion, since committing oneself to acting on universal laws involves an absolute refusal to risk immoral actions, even if they might appear to have a greater expected utility. It is also possible to argue that Kant's universalizability tests—wherein an agent asks whether they could will a maxim of action as a universal law to govern all rational agents—involve capacities for mental time-travel, as universalizability tests might be construed as involving imaginatively simulating a law's potential future causal effects.[38] However, as with Aristotelianism and Utilitarianism, such explanations would at most be retrofitted to the existing behavioral neuroscientific evidence. To the best of my knowledge, no Kantian has ever argued that risk-aversion, mental time-travel, OPT, facial recognition, and fear, sadness, or anxiety are all central to moral cognition—as research on DMN regions implies.

Perhaps more importantly, Kantianism also makes descriptive claims about moral psychology and normative claims about what should be observed in the behavioral psychology of moral agents that either have no empirical support or are in tension with actual findings. For example, Kant famously argued that moral cognition and motivation are located outside of the empirical world, in 'transcendental freedom': a practical capacity to act categorically on maxims irrespective of any psychological inclinations a person may have in the physical world.[39] However, not only is there no empirical evidence of transcendental freedom; a wealth of evidence indicates, to the contrary, that moral behavior is in fact caused by psychological inclinations—namely, the inclinations and brain functions summarized in Chapter 1. Similarly, neo-Kantians argue that morality is cognitively and normatively grounded in constitutive features of agency,[40] reflective endorsement of one's own ends and commitment to one's categorical value as an end-giver,[41] or representation of unconditional goodness.[42] Yet one problem here is that there are ample reasons to doubt whether 'constitutivist' approaches to moral normativity can succeed.[43] A second problem is that the behavioral neuroscience covered in Chapter 1 gives no indication that moral cognition is rooted in constitutive features of agency, reflective endorsement of one's ends, representation of unconditional goodness, and so on. On the contrary, as we have seen the evidence suggests that moral belief and moral sensitivity are rooted in risk-aversion, mental time-travel, OPT, emotional responses, concern for cross-temporal contingencies, and so on—capacities and dispositions that are normatively and descriptively at the heart of this book's theory (Figures 3.1 and 3.2). Further, Kantianism struggles to explain psychopathy. Psychopaths do not appear to be deficient in rational reflection or the ability to understand social moral norms.[44] Instead, as we saw in Chapter 1, they display pronounced deficits in mental time-travel, OPT, risk-aversion, and the ability to use prospective regret to inhibit their behavior—all of the phenomena this book's theory normatively and descriptively roots morality in. None of this disproves Kantian constitutivist approaches to normative moral theory. On the contrary, as I argue in Chapter 5, it may ultimately be possible to conjoin this book's account with a form of Kantian constitutivism. The point for our purposes is that this book's theory appears to be a simpler, more unified, and more explanatorily powerful normative and descriptive explanation of the neuroscientific evidence than Kantianism.

First, Kantianism is based primarily on contentious claims about categorical imperatives, constitutive features of agency, and so on that many theorists question. In contrast, this book's theory is based on a variety of intuitive observations on how prudent and moral people behave and learn (Chapters 2 and 3), which also (as we have just seen) cohere with a growing body of evidence in behavioral neuroscience. This book's theory thus satisfies the principle of Firm Foundations better than Kantianism. It also appears to better satisfy other principles of theory selection, including Parsimony, Unity, and Explanatory Power. For whereas Kantianism splits prudence and morality into two fundamentally different normative and psychological domains (viz. hypothetical versus categorical imperatives), this book's theory holds that moral normativity and cognition are reducible to prudential normativity and cognition. This book's theory is thus a more unified normative and descriptive explanation of morality, one that in turn (as we saw in Chapter 3) appears to normatively unify several leading but traditionally opposed moral frameworks (consequentialism, deontology, contractualism, and virtue ethics), as well as entail a unified theory of political morality (viz. a series of Social-Political Original Positions).

3.2.4 Advantages over Traditional Forms of Contractarianism and Contractualism

Now consider contractarianism, the view that morality normatively reduces to an instrumentally rational social contract, and contractualism, the view that morality reduces to a kind of fair contract. Contractarianism is most famously associated with Hobbes, who argued that instrumentally rational agents have grounds to obey a social contract governed by a number of Laws of Nature that comprise moral norms.[45] Contractarianism also has contemporary defenders, including David Gauthier and Gregory Kavka. Notice how, in a manner of speaking, the theory this book has defended is contractarian. First, I argued that prudence consists in a diachronically rational contract with one's own possible selves (viz. the Prudential Original Position). I then argued that morality is comprised by a more specific diachronic contract between one's present and future selves based on prudential motives to avoid possible regret—which I argued leads rational individuals to treat the possible interests of other persons and sentient beings fairly (viz. the Moral Original Position). In an important sense, then, I believe contractarianism is correct. The relevant question is whether my version of contractarianism is a more attractive normative and descriptive explanation of behavioral neuroscientific evidence than extant versions of contractarianism.

As with other normative moral theories, it is possible to retrofit existing versions of contractarianism to the behavioral neuroscientific evidence. For example, Hobbes, Gauthier, or Kavka could argue that instrumental rationality requires risk-aversion due to mistrust of others (Hobbes) or knowledge that one's own motives are partially transparent to others (Kavka), both of which could lead one to fear violating social moral rules. As such, Hobbesians could also argue that prudential and moral cognition lead agents to be concerned for possible future outcomes (e.g. social punishment), thereby causing prudent moral agents to imagine and care about how other people might react to their behavior. Notice, however, that the more one fills in these details, the more the account simply converges with theory presented in Chapters 2 and 3. This, in my view, is the problem with extant versions of contractarianism. They can only explain the behavioral neuroscientific evidence summarized in Chapter 1 by altering their background assumptions in ways that make them more or less equivalent to this book's theory.

Contractualism, the view that morality is not reducible to prudence but rather a distinctly moral contract, faces more serious explanatory problems. Consider Scanlon's influential version of contractualism, according to which morality consists of acting on principles that no one could reasonably reject.[46] Scanlon's theory may be retrofitted to some of the neuroscience—holding, for example, that OPT may be vital to understand which principles others could reasonably reject. However, Scanlon does not normatively reduce 'reasonable rejectability' to anything more basic, nor does he provide a clear descriptive account of what prudential or moral cognition involve above and beyond grasping one's normative reasons—as he takes normative reasons to be primitive.[47] Scanlon's theory thus provides no clear or detailed normative or descriptive explanation of Chapter 1's behavioral neuroscientific evidence. Thus, this book's theory fares better than Scanlon's theory, normatively and descriptively, on the Seven Principles of Theory Selection. Other contractualist theories do not appear to fare any better. Among other things, critics of contractualism have pointed out that contractualist accounts presuppose moral constraints in setting up conditions for a fair contract—thus leaving the rationality of those moral constraints unexplained.[48]

3.2.5 Advantages over Moral Realism

Finally, consider mind-independent moral realism, a view currently enjoying a great deal of philosophical interest.[49] According to moral realists, moral reasons are primitive. They are not reducible to anything psychological, nor to prudential normative reasons. Compared to moral realism, the explanatory advantages of this book's theory are evident across the Seven Principles of Theory Selection. First, moral realism does not satisfy Firm Foundations, as realist claims that moral reasons are distinctive and primitive are both highly contentious.[50] Second, compared to this book's theory, moral realism is not Parsimonious. Whereas this book's theory normatively and descriptively reduces prudence and morality to moral psychology and instrumental rationality, moral realism posits *non-natural* normative properties irreducible to anything more basic. Third, this book's theory has greater Explanatory Power and Unity. Whereas moral realists hold that moral reasons and prudential reasons are primitive and irreducible to one another—and that neither type of reason is reducible to anything more basic (such as moral psychology)—this book's theory reduces prudence, morality, and political morality to descriptive moral-prudential psychology and our shared normative concept of instrumental rationality. Finally, this book's theory has greater normative and descriptive Fruitfulness, as unlike moral realism it provides a detailed, testable neurofunctional theory of prudential and moral cognition (Figure 3.2), along with a normative theory that promises to resolve a variety of philosophical problems, including but not limited to the unification of competing moral frameworks and solution to the 'problem of overdemandingness'.[51]

3.3 Explanatory Advantages over Alternative Descriptive Theories of Moral Psychology

Let us now turn away from normative theories to empirical theories of moral psychology. Such theories fall broadly into three categories:

- **Rationalist theories**: which hold that moral cognition is based on reasoning and rationality.

- **Sentimentalist theories**: which hold that moral cognition is primarily based on emotion, rather than reasoning or rationality.
- **Hybrid theories**: which hold that that moral cognition and motivation centrally involve both reason and emotion.

We will now see that this book's theory fares better as a normative and descriptive explanation of Chapter 1's behavioral neuroscience than currently influential theories of all three types.

3.3.1 Advantages over Rationalist Theories

We have already examined a number of rationalist normative moral theories: Kantianism, contractarianism and contractualism, and moral realism. In each case, we have seen this book's theory appears to provide a more successful normative and descriptive explanation of a range of evidence. However, Joshua May has recently defended a rationalist account of moral psychology that is more consistent with existing empirical evidence than other rationalist theories discussed above. I think May's theory does a real service not only in showing that moral cognition and motivation involve both reason and emotion, but also the kinds of reasoning and emotion they involve. After all, May recognizes that moral reasoning and motivation involve reasoning about future consequences, OPT, and emotions such as empathy, moral principles, and moral virtues.[52] At the same time, May's project is more limited than this book's. May's primary aim is to rebut moral sentimentalism and skepticism about the role of reason in moral judgment and motivation.[53] May does not aim to provide a descriptive or normative theory of how prudence and morality are related, nor a complete descriptive theory of moral psychology, nor a normative moral theory. Although he does briefly discuss several normative principles—including a consequentialist principle, intentionality principle, and action principle[54] (implying they may be normatively binding because they are so pervasive in moral judgment[55])—there is intuitively an 'is-ought' gap between the descriptive claim that certain moral principles are universal and the further claim that they are normatively justified. For example, Kantians recognize that people tend to care about consequences; Kantians just deny that we *should*, arguing that morality, properly understood, is deontological not consequentialist. More generally, although some values appear to be universal, there is significant disagreement between individuals and groups over which 'moral foundations' are normatively justified.[56]

Consequently, I believe that the right way to conceive May's theory is as consistent with but less detailed (normatively and descriptively) than this book's theory. First, because he does not defend any particular normative moral theory, May does not provide a normative explanation of why moral cognition and motivation should engage all of the capacities examined in Chapter 1. Second, this book's theory normatively and descriptively explains prudence and morality together, in a unified fashion, whereas May focuses only on moral reasoning and motivation. Third, this book's theory promises (as we saw in Chapter 3) to explain how competing moral frameworks (deontology, consequentialism, contractualism, and virtue ethics) can be unified, both normatively (Figure 3.1) and descriptively (via moral cognition, see Figure 3.2). Finally, although May's account might be 'retrofitted' to particular findings summarized in Chapter 1—specifically, to the centrality of risk-aversion, mental-time travel, and OPT (which May might say are involved in reasoning about consequences[57] and self-other merging[58])—May does not provide clear normative grounds or a descriptive mechanism to explain why or how stimulating forward-looking mental time-travel should improve both prudential and moral behavior. In contrast, this book's theory explains how 'moral risk-aversion' leads prudent agents to adopt the perspective of their own possible future selves and the perspectives of others, in accordance with empirical findings.[59] Consequently, although May's theory is consistent with Chapter 1's empirical findings—as well as, in principle, with this book's theory—the present theory promises a more explanatorily powerful and unified normative and descriptive explanation of the behavioral neuroscientific evidence.

3.3.2 Advantages over Sentimentalist Theories

A number of philosophers and psychologists have also defended sentimentalist theories of moral psychology, holding that reason plays little to no role in moral motivation.[60] One prominent sentimentalist theory is Haidt's Social Intuition Model and associated Moral Foundations Theory, which hold that moral judgments are largely based on unreflective emotional reactions that are only rationalized after the fact. However, as May argues, the problem with sentimentalist theories of moral psychology is that they are contradicted by empirical evidence.[61] The behavioral neuroscientific evidence shows that reason is involved in moral behavior: that our reasoned inferences about moral beliefs do motivate us, and that moral judgment and motivation involve rational planning

116 A Unified Neurofunctional Theory?

concerning mental time-travel, risk-aversion, and OPT. For example, psychopaths appear to lack normal judgments and fail to obey moral norms not because they lack specific emotions, but because they do not apply their emotions to future consequences in a rational way—one that prevents them from learning from their prudential and moral mistakes in ways that prudent individuals do.[62] For all intents and purposes, then, sentimentalist theories should be treated as disconfirmed by available evidence.

3.3.3 Advantages over Existing Hybrid Theories

Given the significant obstacles to rationalist and sentimentalist theories of moral psychology, the most promising approach to moral psychology is a hybrid approach: an approach holding that reason and emotion both play central roles in moral belief and motivation. Notice that the theory this book defends is a hybrid theory: it argues that normatively prudent and moral behavior is neurofunctionally caused by cognitive processes (mental time-travel, weighing risk and uncertainty, etc.) and emotional processes (regret for bad decisions, empathy with others via OPT, etc.). The relevant question is whether, of the hybrid theories that exist, this book's theory offers the most compelling explanation of the neuroscientific evidence. Because we cannot compare this book's theory to every alternative, allow me to focus on a couple of prominent ones.

In *Braintrust*, Patricia Churchland argues that *oxytocin*, caring for others, and interpersonal problem-solving capacities are 'the neural platform' for moral behavior. More specifically, she defends a four-dimensional model of moral psychology which holds the following:

> [W]hat we humans call *ethics* or *morality* is shaped by interlocking brain processes: (1) *caring* (rooted in attachment to kin and kith and care for their well-being), (2) *recognition of others' psychological states* (rooted in the benefits of predicting the behavior of others), (3) *problem-solving in a social context* (e.g. how we should distribute scarce goods...), and (4) *learning social practices* (by positive and negative reinforcement, by trial and error, by various kinds of conditioning, and by analogy).[63]

Ultimately, Churchland uses this theory to defend a kind of Aristotelian virtue ethics, arguing that we learn to internalize dispositions to care for others that are mutually beneficial.[64]

A Unified Neurofunctional Theory? 117

There is much to like about Churchland's account. Indeed, if the theory this book defends is correct, several elements of her theory of moral psychology are correct: particularly its focus on (instrumental) problem-solving, social learning, and recognition of others' psychological states. However, there are reasons to believe that the current book's theory is a more successful normative and descriptive explanation of the behavioral neuroscientific evidence.

One problem with Churchland's account is her focus on *oxytocin* and its effects on caring for family members, friends, and the need for attachment. Churchland takes this form of caring, and concern for attachment, to be at the heart of moral psychology. However, although *oxytocin* does increase empathy and trust under certain conditions, Churchland's claim that it lies at the heart of moral cognition sits poorly with a variety of empirical findings. Among other things, *oxytocin* has been found to increase group-serving dishonesty[65] and biases favoring one's own in-groups over outgroups[66]—behaviors that are intuitively immoral, or at best amoral. *Oxytocin* thus seems better described as a source of *tribalism* or caring concern 'for one's own kind' (one's own kin, group, or race), not morality. This is further illustrated by Churchland's point that that nonhuman animals have *oxytocin* responses.[67] Animals' dispositions to care for their young are not full-fledged moral dispositions worthy of praise or blame, but rather seem better described as mere instincts to 'protect their own'.

This raises another deep issue with Churchland's account, which is that it holds that human beings and nonhuman animals both have moral capacities. Although Churchland defends this idea,[68] this conflicts with the fact that we do not treat nonhuman animals as morally responsible agents whose actions warrant moral praise or blame. It further conflicts with the behavioral neuroscientific evidence. As mentioned above, a second plank of Churchland's theory of moral psychology is that morality involves problem-solving and social learning. However, Churchland does not provide a sophisticated account of the neuroscience of problem-solving. She writes, 'The capacity for problem-solving, whatever that really involves in terms of brain-circuitry, allows for the emergence of novel behaviors...'.[69] Later, she focuses on the prefrontal cortex, which has a well-established link to problem-solving,[70] OPT,[71] and imagining the future (viz. mental time-travel)[72]—in short, many of the same capacities that this book's theory takes to be central to prudential and moral cognition.

The vital point that Churchland does not discuss is that human beings appear to be alone in the animal kingdom in possessing robust mental-time-travel capacities.[73] As we have seen, mental time-travel appears to be what distinguishes competent, responsible moral agents from agents with diminished or absent moral capacities, such as psychopaths, children, and adolescents.[74] Consequently, there is ample evidence that it is the cognitive processes that this book's theory places at the center of moral psychology—our mental time-travel capacities to imagine and care about different possible pasts, futures, and presents (viz. the problem of possible future selves)—that comprise the foundation of prudential and moral cognition, as opposed to *oxytocin*.

This book's theory thus appears to be a better normative and descriptive explanation of the behavioral neuroscience. Although the three other planks in Churchland's 'neural platform' for moral psychology appear compelling, one of them (*oxytocin*) is normatively and descriptively doubtful as a moral capacity. In contrast, this book's theory normatively and descriptively reduces prudential and moral behavior to a single, unified neurofunctional process: diachronic prudential reasoning—which provides promising normative and descriptive explanations for the findings reported in Chapter 1.

One final influential hybrid theory of moral psychology is given by Peter Singer and Joshua Greene, who argue that moral cognition involves two systems: a largely unreflective emotional system (generating deontological intuitions) and a more reflective reasoning-based system (generating utilitarian intuitions).[75] This theory appears correct, as far as it goes, and is consistent with the theory of prudence and morality this book has defended. Notice, however, that this book's theory explains notably more: namely, why we have the kinds of emotional responses we do (viz. fear-conditioning in childhood, adolescence, and adulthood supporting 'moral risk-aversion'), and how reason uses those emotional responses (in mental time-travel, OPT, etc.), to balance deontological concerns (coercion-avoidance) against consequences (viz. fair negotiation). Further, this book's theory addresses various empirical findings (the links between risk-aversion, mental time-travel, etc. to moral belief and motivation) that are beyond the scope of Singer's and Greene's accounts. Finally, this book's theory promises more normative explanatory power, including the potential to justify a variety of moral principles and a comprehensive normative account of political morality.

4 Conclusion

This chapter outlined how this book's theory of prudence and morality appears to be a more promising normative and descriptive explanation of behavioral neuroscientific findings than other normative moral theories and descriptive theories of moral psychology, and how the theory defended gives rise to a variety of testable predictions for future empirical research. If this chapter is correct, this book's theory warrants further philosophical and empirical investigation.

Notes

1 Woodward (2017).
2 Baron and Norton (forthcoming), Bertrand (forthcoming).
3 Fogal and Risberg (forthcoming).
4 Väyrynen (2013, forthcoming).
5 Woodward (2017): §1.
6 Sober (1985).
7 See Stanford (2017) for an overview.
8 Hawking and Mlodinow (2011): 41–2.
9 Duhem [1906], Quine (1951), Harding (1976).
10 Williams (2016).
11 Einstein (1940): 490.
12 Gawronski and Bodenhausen (2015), Grobler and Wiśniewski (2005), Laudan (1997), Newman (2010).
13 Huemer (2009), Newman (2010), Roche (2018).
14 Arvan (2016): 13 & Chapter 1, §2.
15 Crockett et al. (2015): 1856.
16 Soutschek et al. (2016), Van Gelder et al. (2013).
17 Birbaumer et al. (2005).
18 Hosking et al. (2017).
19 Decety et al. (2013).
20 Baskin-Sommers et al. (2016).
21 Kochanska et al. (2002), Kohlberg (1973).
22 Carpendale (2000).
23 Ariely and Jones (2012), Batson (2015), Mazar et al. (2008).
24 May (2018): 168.
25 Keltner et al. (2003), Owen and Davidson (2009).
26 Schwitzgebel (2019). Cf. Cialdini et al. (2006).
27 Soutschek et al. (2016).
28 See Stalnaker et al. (2015).
29 Annas (1993), Hursthouse (1999).
30 Blumenthal-Barby (2019), Lott (2014), Matchulat (2014).
31 Mill [1861]: Chapter V.
32 Scheffler (1982).
33 Singer (1972).
34 See Batson (2015).
35 Singer (1972): 232, 236-9.
36 Nagel (1980).
37 Batson (2015), Schwitzgebel (2019). Cf. May (2018): ch 6.
38 Cf. Kant [1785]: 4:403, 4:422–4.
39 Ibid.: Section III.
40 Korsgaard (2009).

41 Markovitz (2014): Chapter 5.
42 Herman (1993).
43 Bukoski (2016, 2017, 2018).
44 Cima *et al.* (2010).
45 Hobbes [1651]: Chapters XIII–XIV.
46 Scanlon (1998).
47 Scanlon (2014).
48 See Ashford and Mulgan (2018): §6 for an overview.
49 Cuneo (2007), Enoch (2011), Parfit (2011), Sayre-McCord (1988), Scanlon (2014), Shafer-Landau (2003).
50 See e.g., Forcehimes and Semrau (2018), Smith (2017).
51 See Chapter 3 of this volume, as well as Arvan (2016): Chapters 6–8.
52 May (2018): Chapters 3, 6, 7, and 9.
53 Ibid.: Chapters 1–2.
54 Ibid..: §§3.2–3.3.
55 Ibid.: §3.4.3.
56 Haidt (2012). Cf. May (2018): §5.3.2, esp. Figure 5.1.
57 May (2018): Chapter 3.
58 Ibid.: Chapter 6.
59 Baskin-Sommers *et al.* (2016), Soutschek *et al.* (2016).
60 Haidt (2001), Nichols (2004), Prinz (2007).
61 May (2018).
62 Baskin-Sommers *et al.* (2016).
63 Churchland (2011): 9.
64 Ibid.: Chapters 6 and 7.
65 Shalvi *et al.* (2014)
66 Stallen *et al.* (2012).
67 Churchland (2011): 14.
68 Ibid.: 23–6.
69 Ibid.: 20.
70 Ibid.: 118–27.
71 Ibid.: 132–54.
72 Ibid.: 131.
73 Suddendorf and Corballis (2007).
74 Arvan (2016): 44–7. See also Chapter 1 of this volume.
75 Singer (2005), Greene (2013).

References

Annas, J. (1993). *The Morality of Happiness*. Oxford: Oxford University Press.

Ariely, D. & Jones, S. (2012). *The (Honest) Truth About Dishonesty: How We Lie to Everyone—Especially Ourselves*. New York, NY: HarperCollins.

Arvan, M. (2016). *Rightness as Fairness: A Moral and Political Theory*. New York: Palgrave MacMillan.

Ashford, E. & Mulgan, T. (2018). Contractualism. In E.N. Zalta (ed.), *The Stanford Encyclopedia of Philosophy*. https://plato.stanford.edu/archives/sum2018/entries/contractualism/.

Baron, S. & Norton, J. (forthcoming). Metaphysical Explanation: The Kitcher Picture. *Erkenntnis*. doi:10.1007/s10670-018-00101-2.

Baskin-Sommers, A., Stuppy-Sullivan, A.M., & Buckholtz, J.W. (2016). Psychopathic Individuals Exhibit But Do Not Avoid Regret during Counterfactual Decision making. *Proceedings of the National Academy of Sciences*, *113*(50), 14438–43.

Batson, D. (2015). *What's Wrong with Morality? A Social-Psychological Perspective*. Oxford: Oxford University Press.

Bertrand, M. (forthcoming). Metaphysical Explanation by Constraint. *Erkenntnis*. doi:10.1007/s10670-018-0009-5.

Birbaumer, N., Veit, R., Lotze, M., Erb, M., Hermann, C., Grodd, W., & Flor, H. (2005). Deficient Fear Conditioning in Psychopathy: A Functional Magnetic Resonance Imaging Study. *Archives of General Psychiatry*, *62*(7), 799–805.

Blumenthal-Barby, J.S. (forthcoming). Dilemmas for the Rarity Thesis in Virtue Ethics and Virtue Epistemology. *Philosophia*, *44*(2), 395–406.

Bukoski, M. (2018). Korsgaard's Arguments for the Value of Humanity. *Philosophical Review*, *127*(2), 197–224.

——— (2017). Self-Validation and Internalism in Velleman's Constitutivism. *Philosophical Studies*, *174*(11), 2667–86.

——— (2016). A Critique of Smith's Constitutivism. *Ethics*, *127*(1), 116–46.

Carpendale, J.I. (2000). Kohlberg and Piaget on Stages and Moral Reasoning. *Developmental Review*, *20*(2), 181–205.

Churchland, P. (2011). *Braintrust: What Neuroscience Tells Us About Morality*. Princeton, NJ: Princeton University Press.

Cialdini, R.B., Demaine, L.J., Sagarin, B.J., Barrett, D.W., Rhoads, K., & Winter, P.L. (2006). Managing Social Norms for Persuasive Impact. *Social Influence*, *1*, 3–15.

Cima, M., Tonnaer, F., & Hauser, M.D. (2010). Psychopaths Know Right from Wrong but Don't Care. *Social Cognitive and Affective Neuroscience*, *5*(1), 59–67.

Crockett, M.J., Siegel, J.Z., Kurth-Nelson, Z., Ousdal, O.T., Story, G., Frieband, C., ... & Dolan, R.J. (2015). Dissociable Effects of Serotonin and Dopamine on the Valuation of Harm in Moral Decision Making. *Current Biology*, *25*(14), 1852–9.

Cuneo, T. (2007). *The Normative Web: An Argument for Moral Realism*. Oxford: Oxford University Press.

Decety, J., Chen, C., Harenski, C., & Kiehl, K.A. (2013). An fMRI Study of Affective Perspective Taking in Individuals with Psychopathy: Imagining Another in Pain Does Not Evoke Empathy. *Frontiers in Human Neuroscience*, *7*(489), doi:10.3389/fnhum.2013.00489.

Duhem, P.M.M [1906]. *The Aim and Structure of Physical Theory*. J. Vuillemin (trans.). Princeton, NJ: Princeton University Press, 1982.

Einstein, A. (1940). The Fundaments of Theoretical Physics. *Science*, *91*(2369), 487–92.

Enoch, D. (2011). *Taking Morality Seriously: A Defense of Robust Realism.* Oxford: Oxford University Press.

Fogal, D. & Risberg, O. (forthcoming). The Metaphysics of Moral Explanations. *Oxford Studies in Metaethics.* https://philpapers.org/archive/FOGTMO.pdf, retrieved 27 June 2019.

Forcehimes, A.T. & Semrau, L. (2018). Are There Distinctively Moral Reasons? *Ethical Theory and Moral Practice, 21*(3), 699–717.

Gawronski, B. & Bodenhausen, G.V. (2015). *Theory and Explanation in Social Psychology.* New York, NY: Guilford Press.

Greene, J. (2013). *Moral Tribes: Emotion, Reason, and the Gap between Us and Them.* New York, NY: Penguin.

Grobler, A. & Wiśniewski, A. (2005). Explanation and Theory Evaluation. *Poznan Studies in the Philosophy of the Sciences and the Humanities, 84*(1), 299–310.

Haidt, J. (2012). *The Righteous Mind: Why Good People Are Divided By Politics and Religion.* New York, NY: Pantheon Books.

────── (2001). The Emotional Dog and its Rational Tail: A Social Intuitionist Approach to Moral Judgment. *Psychological Review, 108*(4), 814–34.

Harding, S. (Ed.). (1976). *Can Theories Be Refuted? Essays on the Duhem-Quine Thesis,* Synthese Library Vol. 81. Dordrecht: D. Reidel Publishing.

Hawking, S. & Mlodinow, L. (2011). *The Grand Design.* New York, NY: Bantam.

Herman, B. (1993). *The Practice of Moral Judgment.* Cambridge, MA: Harvard University Press.

Hobbes, T. [1651]. *Leviathan.* In Sir W. Molesworth (ed.), *The English Works of Thomas Hobbes: Now First Collected and Edited,* Vol. 3. London: John Bohn, 1839–45, ix–714.

Hosking, J.G., Kastman, E.K., Dorfman, H.M., Samanez-Larkin, G.R., Baskin-Sommers, A., Kiehl, K.A., ... Buckholtz, J. W. (2017). Disrupted Prefrontal Regulation of Striatal Subjective Value Signals in Psychopathy. *Neuron, 95*(1), 221–31.

Huemer, M. (2009). When is Parsimony a Virtue? *Philosophical Quarterly, 59*(235), 216–36.

Hursthouse, R. (1999). *On Virtue Ethics.* Oxford: Oxford University Press.

Kant, I. [1785]. *Groundwork of the Metaphysics of Morals.* In M.J. Gregor (ed.), *The Cambridge Edition of the Works of Immanuel Kant: Practical Philosophy.* Cambridge: Cambridge University Press, 1996, 38–108.

Keltner, D., Gruenfeld, D.H., & Anderson, C. (2003). Power, Approach, and Inhibition. *Psychological Review, 110*(2), 265–84.

Kochanska, G., Gross, J.N., Lin, M.H., & Nichols, K.E. (2002). Guilt in Young Children: Development, Determinants, and Relations with a Broader System of Standards. *Child Development, 73,* 461–82.

Kohlberg, L. (1973). The Claim to Moral Adequacy of a Highest Stage of Moral Judgment. *The Journal of Philosophy, 70*(18), 630–46.

Korsgaard, C. (2009). *Self-Constitution: Agency, Identity, and Integrity.* Oxford: Oxford University Press.
Laudan, L. (1997). How About Bust? Factoring Explanatory Power Back into Theory Evaluation. *Philosophy of Science, 64*(2), 306–16.
Lott, M. (2014). Situationism, Skill, and the Rarity of Virtue. *Journal of Value Inquiry, 48*(3), 387–401.
Markovitz, J. (2014). *Moral Reason.* Oxford: Oxford University Press.
Matchulat, J. (2014). Defending Virtue against the Situationist Challenge. *Proceedings of the American Catholic Philosophical Association, 88,* 245–58.
May, J. (2018). *Regard for Reason in the Moral Mind.* Oxford: Oxford University Press.
Mazar, N., Amir, O., & Ariely, D. (2008). The Dishonesty of Honest People: A Theory of Self-Concept Maintenance. *Journal of Marketing Research, 45*(6), 633–44.
Mill, J.S. [1861]. *Utilitarianism.* Reprinted in G. Sher (ed.), *Utilitarianism: and the 1868 Speech on Capital Punishment.* Indianapolis: Hackett, 2001.
Nagel, T. (1980). The Limits of Objectivity. *The Tanner Lectures on Human Values, 1,* 75–139.
Newman, M. (2010). Beyond Structural Realism: Pluralist Criteria for Theory Evaluation. *Synthese, 174*(3), 413–43.
Nichols, S. (2004). *Sentimental Rules: On the Natural Foundations of Moral Judgment.* Oxford: Oxford University Press.
Owen, D. & Davidson, J. (2009). Hubris Syndrome: An Acquired Personality Disorder? A Study of US Presidents and UK Prime Ministers Over the Last 100 Years. *Brain, 132*(5), 1396–406.
Parfit, D. (2011). *On What Matters, Vols. 1&2.* Oxford: Oxford University Press.
Prinz, J. (2006). The Emotional Basis of Moral Judgments. *Philosophical Explorations, 9*(1), 29–43.
Quine, W.V.O. (1951). Two Dogmas of Empiricism. *The Philosophical Review, 60*(1), 20–43.
Roche, W. (2018). The Perils of Parsimony. *Journal of Philosophy, 115*(9), 485–505.
Sayre-McCord, G. (ed.) (1988). *Essays on Moral Realism.* Ithaca, NY: Cornell University Press.
Scanlon, T.M. (2014). *Being Realistic About Reasons.* Oxford: Oxford University Press.
——— (1998). *What We Owe to Each Other.* Cambridge, MA: Harvard University Press.
Scheffler, S. (1982). *The Rejection of Consequentialism.* Oxford: Clarendon Press.
Schwitzgebel, E. (2019). Aiming for Moral Mediocrity. *Res Philosophica, 96*(3), 347–68.
Shafer-Landau, R. (2003). *Moral Realism: A Defence.* Oxford: Oxford University Press.

Shalvi S. & De Dreu C.K. (2014). Oxytocin Promotes Group-Serving Dishonesty. *Proceedings of the National Academy of Sciences of the United States of America*, *111*(15), 5503–7.
Singer, P. (2005). Ethics and Intuitions. *The Journal of Ethics*, *9*, 331–52.
——— (1972). Famine, Affluence, and Morality. *Philosophy and Public Affairs*, *1*(3), 229–43.
Smith, M (2017). Parfit's Mistaken Meta-Ethics. In P. Singer (ed.), *Does Anything Really Matter? Essays on Parfit and Objectivity*. Oxford: Oxford University Press, 99–120.
Sober, E. (1985) Panglossian Functionalism and the Philosophy of Mind. *Synthese*, *64*, 165–93.
Soutschek, A., Ruff, C.C., Strombach, T., Kalenscher, T., & Tobler, P.N. (2016). Brain Stimulation Reveals Crucial Role of Overcoming Self-Centeredness in Self-control. *Science Advances*, *2*(10), e1600992.
Stallen, M., De Dreu, C.K., Shalvi, S., Smidts, A., & Sanfey, A.G. (2012). The Herding Hormone: Oxytocin Stimulates In-Group Conformity. *Psychological Science*, *23*(11), 1288–92.
Stalnaker, T.A., Cooch, N.K., & Schoenbaum, G. (2015). What the Orbitofrontal Cortex Does Not Do. *Nature Neuroscience*, *18*(5), 620–7.
Stanford, K. (2017). Underdetermination of Scientific Theory. In E.N. Zalta (ed.) *The Stanford Encyclopedia of Philosophy*. https://plato.stanford.edu/archives/win2017/entries/scientific-underdetermination/.
Suddendorf, T. & Corballis, M.C. (2007). The Evolution of Foresight: What is Mental Time Travel, and is it Unique to Humans? *Behavioral and Brain Sciences*, *30*(3), 299–313.
Van Gelder, J.L., Hershfield, H.E., & Nordgren, L.F. (2013). Vividness of the Future Self Predicts Delinquency. *Psychological Science*, 24(6), 974–80.
Väyrynen, P. (2019). Reasons Why in Normative Explanation. *Inquiry: An Interdisciplinary Journal of Philosophy*, *62*(6), 607–23.
——— (2013). Grounding and Normative Explanation. *Aristotelian Society Supplementary Volume*, *87*(1), 155–78.
Williams, M. (2016). What is the Geocentric Model of the Universe? *Universe Today*. https://www.universetoday.com/32607/geocentric-model/, retrieved 28 May 2019.
Woodward, J. (2017). Scientific Explanation. In E.N. Zalta (ed.), *The Stanford Encyclopedia of Philosophy*. https://plato.stanford.edu/archives/fall2017/entries/scientific-explanation/.

5 Replies to Potential Concerns, and Avenues for Future Research

This book outlined a novel theory of prudence in Chapter 2. It then showed how that theory entails a theory of morality (Rightness as Fairness) in Chapter 3 and demonstrated in Chapter 4 how this unified theory of prudence and morality currently appears to offer the most compelling normative and descriptive explanation of the behavioral neuroscientific evidence outlined in Chapter 1. However, readers may have residual concerns. Although I cannot address every concern here, my hope is that my responses to several likely ones will further establish the importance of pursuing future empirical and philosophical work on this book's project.

1 Concern #1: Too Speculative?

One potential concern is that this book's theory is speculative. First, it is normatively speculative. Is the theory correct about what prudence normatively requires, and how morality can be normatively derived from prudence? Second, the theory is empirically speculative. Do human prudential and moral cognition and motivation really function in the ways theorized?

My response is that well-founded speculation of the sort this book has engaged in can be important and has been historically fruitful. For example, although Darwin did not have modern molecular biology at his disposal, his speculations about evolution by natural selection based on field observations, geology, and other evidence established the importance of investigating the theory of evolution further.[1] Similarly, Einstein's speculations in 1905 and 1915 about relativity[2] were highly fruitful, even though it was not until 1919 that Eddington confirmed the theory's predictions about bending starlight.[3] I do not intend (by any means) to compare this book's theory to these groundbreaking works. The point is simply that these and other similar cases illustrate how well-founded speculation can be important—and that what should matter, at least in the short run, is whether a theory makes a strong case that its speculations are likely to be fruitful. I submit that this book has accomplished this, as Chapter 4 argued that the theory of prudence and morality defended here currently satisfies Seven Principles of Theory Selection better than alternatives. Further, unlike many prominent normative moral theories, which as we saw in Chapter 4 do not make clear predictions about moral psychology, this book's theory makes clear empirical predictions (Figures 2.5 and 3.1). The theory can thus be empirically tested.

2 Concern #2: The Is-Ought Gap and Naturalistic Fallacy

Many have argued that normative moral philosophy and descriptive moral psychology are fundamentally distinct, and that empirical science can have nothing fruitful to say about normative matters. For example, G.E. Moore famously alleged that it is always fallacious to attempt to identify the good with any natural property, such as what is pleasant or desired.[4] Similarly, Hume and many others allege there is an 'is-ought gap'[5]—that what normatively ought to be can never be derived purely from descriptive premises about what is. These ideas remain influential.[6]

I cannot refute the naturalistic fallacy or is-ought gap here. However, allow me to say two brief things in reply. First, this book's theory does not presuppose that the normative is reducible to the descriptive. Chapter 2's theory of prudence was based on normative theorizing about the kinds of actions and internalized dispositions that have the best-expected long-term outcomes for agents, *vis-à-vis* instrumental normativity. Chapter 2 then developed a descriptive theory of prudential psychology based on empirical observations of how prudential cognition appears to function. Chapter 3 then extrapolated a normative theory of morality and descriptive theory of moral psychology from Chapter 2's arguments. Consequently, the theory does not presuppose that normativity is reducible to any natural property, nor does it deny that there may be an 'is-ought gap'. The normative elements of this book's theory have been defended on *normative* grounds, and its descriptive elements on *descriptive* grounds.

Second, although the theory does not presuppose that the naturalistic fallacy and is-ought gap are false, I am optimistic that both views are false, and that this book's theory can be conjoined with arguments that may establish this. A number of theorists (including myself) have argued against the naturalistic fallacy and is-ought gap, contending that normativity (and, by extension, morality) can be reduced to descriptive, naturalistic facts about what is.[7] My own favored account is that the normative can be reduced to a descriptive social-psychological account of normative semantics.[8] I contend, first, that normative concepts such as 'ought', 'good', and 'bad' are purely descriptive psychological phenomena, as they are simply concepts represented in or otherwise processed by the brain. I then argue that the 'satisfaction-conditions' of normative concepts reduce to psychosocial dispositions: dispositions shared by language-users to say and judge when the concepts apply 'correctly' or 'incorrectly'. As an illustration, consider the instrumental use of the normative concept 'good'. Competent language users such as you and I say and judge that an action is 'good' in an instrumental sense when and only when it best satisfies the relevant agent's ends—thus illustrating how the truth-conditions and truthmakers of normative propositions can both be identified with purely descriptive, naturalistic facts.

To see why this kind of 'Humean reduction' of the normative to descriptive may be compelling, consider a person playing chess. On the psychosocial account of normative semantics I advocate, when we say to someone playing a game of chess, 'That is a good move', we may be uttering a true normative proposition: namely, the proposition that the person *is* (instrumentally) making a good move. Nevertheless, the truth-conditions and truthmaker for this proposition on my favored account are both purely descriptive: we say and judge it to be true that 'X is a good move' (a descriptive fact about linguistic behavior) when and only when, as a descriptive empirical fact, the move is likely to help win the game. Hence, on my favored account, all of normativity—the sense in which normative propositions express normative truths (viz. 'oughts')—may indeed be reduced to purely descriptive, naturalistic facts about what *is*.

Of course, 'Humean reductions' of normativity to the descriptive like this are controversial. The point is simply that these are matters for further debate, not grounds for rejecting this book's project. For again, neither component of this book's theory—neither its normative theory of prudence and morality nor its associated descriptive model of prudential and moral cognition—presupposes that such a reduction is correct.

3 Concern #3: Prudence Without 'Moral Risk-Aversion'?

Chapter 2 argued that prudent agents typically internalize a specific form of 'moral risk-aversion' across childhood, adolescence, and adulthood. Specifically, I argued that prudent agents typically learn by adulthood to internalize (1) negative attitudes to categorically avoid risking immoral behavior and (2) positive attitudes to categorically act morally 'for its own sake'. However, are these attitudes and the actions they normatively require (i.e. Rightness as Fairness) always prudent? There are plausible reasons for doubt. There seem to be extreme 'moral risk-takers' in our midst—that is, individuals who routinely run the risk of violating moral norms—who seem to live prudentially successful lives, such as powerful political or business leaders who repeatedly violate moral norms to their own benefit. The worry here is that if there exist individuals for whom 'moral risk-aversion' is not prudent, then my theory of prudence is either false or limited in application, and my theory of morality's normative rationality (viz. Rightness as Fairness) is similarly false or limited.

Although I am uncertain which response to this concern is ultimately correct, my hope is that each response I provide below is promising, though I concede that some are disturbing.

First, one possibility is that although some people—particularly those with great power—may be able to benefit tremendously from violating moral norms in the short- or medium-term, they are still plausibly taking imprudent risks concerning their life as a whole. As we saw in Chapters 2 and 3, it is all too easy to give a long list of powerful people in history who seemed to benefit tremendously from immoral behavior over years or even decades, only to unexpectedly suffer personal prudential catastrophe many years later as a result. For example, although the ancient Athenian leader Pericles enjoyed fame, fortune, and power for many years, he ended up dying a horrible death and seeing Athens fall into ruin as a result of him recklessly waging a (morally and prudentially) risky war against Sparta.[9] Pericles is far from alone. History is littered with powerful people who risked violating moral norms, only to suffer highly regrettable long-term outcomes: Hitler, Mussolini, Saddam Hussein, Muammar al-Gaddafi, Richard Nixon, Ken Lay and Jeff Skilling of ENRON, and Bernie Madoff are just a few names that immediately come to mind. Although violating moral norms 'paid off' in the short to medium run in these (and many other) cases, the individuals' decisions still seem imprudent, for roughly the very same reasons that children, adolescents, and most adults learn that immorality is imprudent: namely, that life is so uncertain that risking immoral behavior is a bad long-term bet.

Consequently, this is my first response to the concern that there are potential counterexamples to my theory of prudence: namely, that they may only be apparent counterexamples. Some people may profit from immoral behavior over the short to medium run, and some may have so much power or luck that they never 'pay' for immoral behavior. Nevertheless, I think it is plausible to argue that 'moral risk-taking' as such is still imprudent because (A) it only takes one mistake for the behavior to end in long-term prudential tragedy, and (B) numerous historical and everyday examples illustrate how it *is* a bad life-policy given just how uncertain life is as a whole.

However, maybe this is overly optimistic. Perhaps it is really prudent for some individuals to sometimes risk violating moral norms or never internalize 'moral risk-aversion' as attitudinal constraints on their first-order life decisions. While I hope neither of these things is true, I am inclined to think that they are ultimately empirical questions, and if they turn out to be true then we should accept their normative consequences, as disturbing as they might be. I have argued that moral philosophy should not presuppose that morality is how we want it to be.[10] Although we may want morality to be categorically binding on all rational agents or think that morality must be categorically binding on everyone,[11] I think we must follow our actual normative and descriptive evidence. If this book is correct—if, as Chapter 4 argued, this book's theory is currently the most compelling normative and descriptive explanation for various phenomena—then we should follow its normative implications wherever they lead. Many true theories in history—ranging from the Copernican theory that the Earth is not the center of the Universe to the theories of evolution and relativity—ultimately overthrew what many people wanted to believe or thought must be true as a matter of 'simple common sense'.[12] If the metaphilosophical approach I defend is correct—that moral philosophy should be based on Seven Principles of Theory Selection rather than traditional philosophical methods—then we must be prepared to revise what we normatively take morality to be.

Further, there are independent normative philosophical and empirical grounds for thinking that the normative limits of this book's theory—its insistence the moral normativity is rooted in and reducible to prudential instrumental concern—corresponds to normative reality. First, consider a popular-culture example I examined in *Rightness as Fairness*: the hypothetical case of the Kelvans, a race of alien beings who can 'freeze' human beings and behave immorally toward humans with absolute impunity for their own benefit.[13] It is very striking how, in the television episode where this case occurred, the Kelvans flatly ignored or dismissed human beings' moral claims, seeing no reason at all to behave morally. Moral philosophers who hold that morality is categorically binding on all rational agents must hold that although the Kelvans can accomplish every goal they have through immoral means, the Kelvans really ought to act morally. One can of course argue this. However, this book's theory implies a far simpler normative explanation: that because the Kelvans have no grounds for moral risk-aversion, the Kelvans were *right*: they really had no normative grounds to behave morally, unless and until it was possible for their absolute power to wane, giving them to have reasons to worry about potential future consequences they might regret. Importantly, this is exactly what happens in the television episode in question: the Kelvans become corrupted by human emotions, learning they can come to regret their immoral behavior—the very mechanism (potential future regret) that this book's theory argues lies at the root of moral risk-aversion (viz. minimax regret) and moral normativity. Although normative moral philosophers may not like these implications, this book's theory explains precisely why the Kelvans found morality to 'have no normative teeth' (or normative persuasiveness) until they developed human-like uncertainty about the future. Second, although the Kelvans are just a hypothetical example, recent empirical results paint a startlingly similar picture. People with pronounced power over others have been found to experience significantly less normative pull of moral norms, engaging in higher levels of risk-taking and moral violations, and demonstrating inhibited abilities to adopt and care about other people's perspectives and interests[14]—so much so that there is an even a name for it: 'Hubris syndrome'.[15] The Kelvan example and Hubris Syndrome together suggest that morality may indeed be experienced as normatively binding only to the extent that we (instrumentally) worry about the possibility of regretting immoral behavior—exactly as this book's theory predicts.

Finally, as disturbing as these implications may be (if borne out empirically)—that morality may only be binding on those for whom moral risk-aversion is rational—this may be practically (indeed morally) important for those of us who have internalized moral risk-aversion to *accept* rather than deny and try to explain away. For suppose it is the case that people with extreme power have no normative grounds to behave morally. In that case, it may be morally and prudentially counterproductive for those of us who have internalized moral motives to insist that such individuals 'really do' have normative grounds to behave morally, for that may blind us to the simple (potential) truth that they really don't. Recognizing and accepting this normative fact (if indeed it is supported by empirical science) may be vital for two reasons. First, it may lead us to better recognize that we must prevent people from gaining immense power over others: that we cannot expect people to feel the normative pull of morality when they have great power, and that we should instead always seek to ensure that people face 'checks and balances' or other forms of moral-social accountability. Second, it may lead us to better recognize that we must provide people and the collectives they comprise (businesses, countries, etc.) with prudential reasons to behave morally, impressing upon them not 'moral principles' (which empirical science indicates carry comparatively little motivating force[16]), but instead Chapter 2's two prudential lessons: that immorality is not worth the risk of immense regret, and morality has better long-term expected benefits, at least if you are patient. It is not difficult to imagine just how many morally and prudentially tragic situations—ranging from slavery and the US Civil War to the Holocaust, World War II, and Watergate—might have never occurred had the individuals and groups involved better recognized that their immoral actions were not only harmful to others but also imprudent, against their own long-term interests.

In sum, given just how many powerful people in history have ended up paying dearly for immoral behavior in the long run, I think it is plausible that this book's account of prudence is indeed prudent for everyone, given the immense uncertainty of life as a whole. At the same time, however, this book's theory allows that *if* there exist legitimate outliers—individuals for whom 'moral risk-aversion' is not prudent—then we should take these normative implications seriously. Understanding and accepting these implications (if they are real, and hopefully rare) may be vital for avoiding 'normative wishful thinking', for developing more effective approaches to moral education, and for adopting more effective social and political policies and norms for incentivizing moral behavior on prudential grounds.

4 Objection #4: Prudence, Not *Morality*?

One final concern is that even if this book's theory is normatively and descriptively accurate, it is not ultimately a theory of morality *per se*, but at most a theory of how morality is prudent. This type of concern dates back at least to Kant, who argued that it is a mistake to try to reduce morality to prudence on the grounds that moral commands are by nature *categorical*, obligating all rational agents irrespective of our sensible (prudential) interests.[17] H.A. Prichard famously defended similar concerns, holding that arguments for moral behavior rooted in self-interest can at most motivate moral behavior, not normatively justify it.[18] These ideas remain influential, with some going so far as to argue that the categorical nature of morality is a 'non-negotiable' feature of moral discourse.[19] Allow me to offer several replies in response.

First, as noted above, I have previously argued that we should be skeptical of intuitive appeals to what people think morality is or want it to be.[20] Morality may seem as though it must be categorically normatively binding, irrespective of what is prudent. However, similar 'seemings' have often turned out to be false. For example, the Earth seems flat, and space and time seem absolute—yet they are not. Because 'seemings' can be false, I argue that moral philosophy should answer to more objective foundations used in empirical science: namely, the Seven Principles of Theory Selection discussed in Chapter 4. Insofar as Chapter 4 argued that this book's theory promises to satisfy those principles better than alternatives, my contention is that this book should encourage philosophers who are inclined to regard prudence and morality as distinct to consider *reconceptualizing* morality as reducing to prudence.

Second, a variety of theorists, ranging from Anscombe, to Foot, Goldman, Joyce, Markovitz, and Williams, have long argued that moral reasons are not truly categorical.[21] As Anscombe famously notes,[22] the idea that there are distinctively moral reasons (independent of prudential ones) appears to be a relatively recent invention in human history—one that may be little more than a conceptual relic of the law-based conception of ethics found in Judeo-Christian religion.[23] Indeed, if one looks at Plato's moral philosophy, or Aristotle's, or the Stoics', and so on, one does not see arguments that morality is 'categorically binding' in a Kantian sense. Rather, one often comes across forms of moral skepticism based on prudential concerns, such as Thrasymachus's argument in Book I of *The Republic* and Polus's argument in *Gorgias* that powerful individuals have no reason to behave 'justly' because of their ability to achieve their ends through unjust means. Similarly, one often comes across elaborate arguments attempting to show how morality is a matter of prudence—for instance, Socrates's arguments about the happiness of a just soul in *Republic* Books IV and IX, Aristotle's arguments in the *Nichomachean Ethics* that moral virtue is necessary for *eudaimonia*, and so on. One also finds similar arguments throughout religious texts, such as the Old Testament's books of Wisdom, Psalms, and Wisdom of Ben Sira, which systematically trumpet the prudential benefits of 'moral behavior' and emphasize the prudential dangers of defying God's (moral) commandments, due to the possibility of divine reward and punishment (respectively). Finally, Forcehimes and Semrau have recently given a powerful argument (in my view) against the idea that there are distinctively moral reasons (reasons different in kind from other reasons).[24]

Third, as influential as the notion of morality's 'categoricity' may be, genuine categorical normatively has proven very difficult to substantiate. For while there are many arguments for categorical normativity,[25] none of them appear to enjoy widespread acceptance.[26] Consequently, there is, I believe, a deep epistemic danger of confirmation bias here: of assuming that morality must be the way we want it to be (i.e. truly categorical), even if our evidence (as this book has argued) points in a different direction.[27]

Fourth, although this book's theory does not justify 'genuine' categorical normativity—that is, moral requirements that are normatively binding irrespective of individuals' contingent psychological interests—this book's theory justifies something very close to it. For as we saw across Chapters 2 and 3, my theory holds that prudent individuals typically internalize 'categorical' commitments to always avoid immoral behavior and behave morally 'for its own sake', even when it might appear not to be in their best interest. On my account, prudent agents come to have 'categorical' moral commitments—and in turn obey principles of fairness that are 'categorically' justifiable to every possible human and nonhuman sentient being in a Moral Original Position—not because there are genuinely categorical normative requirements, but instead because it is *prudent* to become the kind of person whose attitudes treat moral principles this way. As we saw in Chapter 4, these claims cohere with scientific findings on moral development and motivation.[28]

Finally, I actually believe that it may be possible to conjoin the account I have provided here with an account of genuinely categorical normative reasons. Although I must leave these matters for another day, I have argued elsewhere that a Kantian constitutivist approach to categorical normativity—one that derives genuinely categorical requirements from constitutive features of agency—converges with this book's theory: specifically, with the Categorical-Instrumental Imperative and Rightness as Fairness.[29] For, as we saw in Chapter 3 and this chapter, there are many parallels between this book's prudential theory of morality and Kant's categorical imperative. This book's theory approximates a kind of 'categoricity' by holding that prudence typically requires acting in ways that one can justify to all of one's possible future selves, and by extension, to all possible human and nonhuman beings one might care about. The difference between this book's project and traditional Kantian ethics is that this book derives 'categorical moral justification' in a new way: a way that promises to unify morality with prudence and empirical neuroscientific evidence. Consequently, although I think it is an important project to examine whether and to what extent this book's theory converges with a truly categorical analysis of morality, we must leave these matters for future investigation.

5 Conclusion

Chapter 1 gave an overview of the emerging behavioral neuroscience of moral and prudential cognition. Chapter 2 then outlined a novel theory of prudence, showing how it coheres with lived experience, including how certain forms of 'moral risk-aversion' are typically learned and reinforced throughout childhood, adolescence, and adulthood. Chapter 3 then showed how this normative and descriptive theory of prudence entails a normative and descriptive psychological theory of morality, Rightness as Fairness. Chapter 4 then argued that this unified theory is currently the most compelling normative and descriptive explanation of the behavioral neuroscientific evidence summarized in Chapter 1, as judged according to Seven Principles of Theory Selection. Finally, this chapter addressed potential concerns, arguing that the theory withstands them.

This book's theory may or may not be correct, either in part or in whole. However, I believe this book has provided compelling reasons for investigating the theory further, both philosophically and empirically. Finally, insofar as some theorists allege that normative philosophical theorizing and empirical psychology are fundamentally distinct,[30] my hope is that this book has provided ample reasons for thinking the contrary: that normative philosophy and empirical neuroscience have much to offer each other, in ways that promise to push both fields in vital new directions.

Notes

1. Darwin [1859]: Chapters I–IV.
2. Einstein (1905, 1915).
3. Dyson *et al.* (1919).
4. Moore [1903].
5. Hume [1739]: 335.
6. See Silliman and Braden-Johnson (2018), Sinclair (2018), Singer (2015), Cf. Parfit (2011), Scanlon (1998, 2014).
7. Jackson (1988), Kohlberg (1971), MacIntyre (1981).
8. Arvan (2016): 28–9.
9. Thucydides [1972].
10. Arvan (2016): Chapter 2, §4.
11. Joyce (2007), Kant [1785], Luco (2016).
12. See Brian (1996): 100–4, 113, Clark (1984): 135–41.
13. *Star Trek: The Original Series* (1968).
14. Galinsky *et al.* (2008).
15. Owen and Davidson (2009).
16. See Batson (2015): 104–5, 108, 119–20. Cf. May (2018): Chapter 6.
17. Kant [1785]: Section III, Kant [1788], Kant [1797]: Introduction, §III.
18. Prichard (1912).
19. Joyce (2007), Luco (2016).
20. Arvan (2016): Chapter 2, §4.
21. Anscombe (1958), Foot (1972), Goldman (2009), Joyce (2007), Markovitz (2014), Williams (1981: 101–4; 1995).
22. Anscombe (1958): 1, 4–13.
23. Ibid.: esp. 1, 4–5.
24. Forcehimes and Semrau (2018).
25. Baron (1995), Herman (1993), Kant [1785, 1797], Korsgaard (2008, 2009), Markovitz (2014): Chapter 5, Wood (2008).
26. See Arvan (2016): 24–7, Joyce (2007): §2.0, §4.3. For some persuasive arguments against several influential approaches to justifying (categorical) moral requirements, see Bukoski (2016, 2017, 2018), Lang (2012), and Smith (2017).
27. Arvan (2016): 10–13.
28. Ariely and Jones (2012), Batson (2015), Kochanska *et al.* (2002), Kohlberg (1973).
29. Arvan (unpublished manuscript).
30. Parfit (2011), Scanlon (1998, 2014).

References

Anscombe, G.E.M. (1958). Modern Moral Philosophy. *Philosophy*, *33*(124), 1–19.

Ariely, D. & Jones, S. (2012). *The (Honest) Truth About Dishonesty: How We Lie to Everyone–Especially Ourselves*. New York, NY: HarperCollins.

Arvan, M. (2016). *Rightness as Fairness: A Moral and Political Theory*. New York: Palgrave MacMillan.

——— (unpublished manuscript). Reformulating the Categorical Imperative.

Baron, M. (1995). *Kantian Ethics Almost Without Apology*. Ithaca: Cornell University Press.
Batson, D. (2015). *What's Wrong with Morality? A Social-Psychological Perspective*. Oxford: Oxford University Press.
Brian, D. (1996). *Einstein: A Life*. New York: John Wiley & Sons, Inc.
Bukoski, M. (2018). Korsgaard's Arguments for the Value of Humanity. *Philosophical Review, 127*(2), 197–224.
——— (2017). Self-Validation and Internalism in Velleman's Constitutivism. *Philosophical Studies, 174*(11), 2667–86.
——— (2016). A Critique of Smith's Constitutivism. *Ethics, 127*(1), 116–46.
Clark, R.W. (1984). *The Survival of Charles Darwin*. New York: Random House.
Darwin, C. [1859]. *The Origin of Species: By Means of Natural Selection of the Preservation of Favoured Races in the Struggle for Life*. New York: New American Library, 1958.
Dyson, F.W., Eddington, A.S., & Davidson, C. (1920). A Determination of the Deflection of Light by the Sun's Gravitational Field, from Observations Made at the Total Eclipse of May 29, 1919. *Philosophical Transactions of the Royal Society of London. Series A, Containing Papers of a Mathematical or Physical Character, 220*, 291–333.
Einstein, A. (1915). The Field Equations of Gravitation. *Sitzung der physikalische-mathematischen Klasse, 25*, 844–47.
——— (1905). On the Electrodynamics of Moving Bodies. *Annalen der Physik, 17*, 891–921.
Foot, P. (1972). Morality as a System of Hypothetical Imperatives. *Philosophical Review, 81*(3), 305–16.
Forcehimes, A.T. & Semrau, L. (2018). Are There Distinctively Moral Reasons? *Ethical Theory and Moral Practice, 21*(3), 699–717.
Galinsky, A.D., Maddux, W.W., Gilin, D., & White, J.B. (2008). Why It Pays to Get Inside the Head of Your Opponent: The Differential Effects of Perspective Taking and Empathy in Negotiations. *Psychological Science, 19*(4), 378–84.
Goldman, A.H. (2009). *Reasons from Within*. Oxford: Oxford University Press.
Herman, B. (1993). *The Practice of Moral Judgment*. Cambridge, MA: Harvard University Press.
Hume, D. [1739]. *A Treatise of Human Nature: Being an Attempt to Introduce the Experimental Method of Reasoning into Moral Subjects*. Vol I–II. London: John Noon.
Jackson, F. (1998). *From Metaphysics to Ethics: A Defence of Conceptual Analysis*. Oxford: Clarendon.
Joyce, R. (2007). *The Myth of Morality*. Cambridge, UK: Cambridge University Press.
Kant, I. [1797]. *The Metaphysics of Morals*. In M.J. Gregor (ed.), *The Cambridge Edition of the Works of Immanuel Kant: Practical Philosophy*. Cambridge: Cambridge University Press, 1996, 353–604.

―― [1788]. *Critique of Practical Reason*, in Ibid., 133–271.
―― [1785]. *Groundwork of the Metaphysics of Morals*, in Ibid., 38–108.
Kochanska, G., Gross, J.N., Lin, M.H., & Nichols, K.E. (2002). Guilt in Young Children: Development, Determinants, and Relations with a Broader System of Standards. *Child Development*, 73, 461–82.
Kohlberg, L. (1973). The Claim to Moral Adequacy of a Highest Stage of Moral Judgment. *The Journal of Philosophy*, 70(18), 630–46.
―― (1971). *From Is to Ought: How to Commit the Naturalistic Fallacy and Get Away with It in the Study of Moral Development*. New York: Academic Press.
Korsgaard, C.M. (2009). *Self-Constitution: Agency, Identity, and Integrity*. Oxford: Oxford University Press.
―― (2008). *The Constitution of Agency*. Oxford: Oxford University Press.
Lang, G. (2012). What's the Matter? Review of Derek Parfit, On What Matters. *Utilitas*, 24(2), 300–12.
Luco, A.C. (2016). Non-Negotiable: Why Moral Naturalism Cannot Do Away with Categorical Reasons. *Philosophical Studies*, 173(9), 2511–28.
MacIntyre, A. (1981). *After Virtue: A Study in Moral Theory*. South Bend: University of Notre Dame Press.
Markovitz, J. (2014). *Moral Reason*. Oxford: Oxford University Press.
May, J. (2018). *Regard for Reason in the Moral Mind*. Oxford: Oxford University Press.
Moore, G.E. [1903]. *Principia Ethica*. New York: Cambridge University Press.
Owen, D. & Davidson, J. (2009). Hubris Syndrome: An Acquired Personality Disorder? A Study of US Presidents and UK Prime Ministers over the Last 100 Years. *Brain*, 132(5), 1396–406.
Parfit, D. (2011). *On What Matters, Vols. 1 & 2*. Oxford: Oxford University Press.
Prichard, H.A. (1912). Does Moral Philosophy Rest on a Mistake? *Mind*, 21, 21–37.
Scanlon, T.M. (2014). *Being Realistic About Reasons*. Oxford: Oxford University Press.
―― (1998). *What We Owe to Each Other*. Cambridge, MA: Harvard University Press.
Silliman, M. & Braden-Johnson, D.K. (2018). Doing Justice to the Is-Ought Gap. *Social Philosophy Today*, 34, 117–32.
Sinclair, N. (2018). The Naturalistic Fallacy and the History of Metaethics. In N. Sinclair (ed.), *The Naturalistic Fallacy*, Cambridge: Cambridge University Press, 9–29.
Singer, D.J. (2015). Mind the Is-Ought Gap. *Journal of Philosophy*, 112(4), 193–210.
Smith, M. (2017). Parfit's Mistaken Meta-ethics. In P. Singer (ed.), *Does Anything Really Matter?: Essays on Parfit and Objectivity*. Oxford: Oxford University Press, 99–120.

Star Trek: The Original Series (1968). By Any Other Name. https://www.imdb.com/title/tt0796366/, retrieved 31 July 2019.

Thucydides [1972]. *History of the Peloponnesian War*. London: Penguin Classics.

Williams, B. (1995). Internal Reasons and the Obscurity of Blame. In *Making Sense of Humanity*. Cambridge: Cambridge University Press, 35–45.

——— (1981). *Moral Luck*. Cambridge: Cambridge University Press.

Wood, A. (2008). *Kantian Ethics*. Cambridge: Cambridge University Press.

Index

Note: *Italic* page numbers refer to figures and page numbers followed by n refer to notes.

abortion 80–2
affective forecasting 29–30
agency 14, 68, 110–11, 134
agreement 31, 62–5, 67, 69–71, 74, 78–9, 82, 85–8, 90n26; *see also* consensus; negotiation
altruism 14, 26, 63–4, 69, 77–9, 105, 109
amygdala 13, 103–4, 107
anger 13, 63, 104
angular gyrus 12, 97, 103
animals 9, 66, 71, 85, 90n26, 117
anxiety 11, 13, *44*, 48–9, 51, 87, *88*, 89n8, 104, 110, 130
Aristotle 1, 28, 132–3
Aristotelianism 100, 106–8, 109, 116; *see also* virtue ethics
attitudes: categorical 42–6, 49–*50*, 75, *86*, *88*, 133; of conscience *41*–3, *50*–1, *88*; cultural 81; of normatively moral agents 61, 68–74, 76–7, 81, *86*–*8*, 102; other-regarding 63–5, *86*; of prudent agents 5n17, 6n18; 36–54n41, 60, 74, 76, *86*–*8*, 128; selfish 63, 77–8; standing 27; toward expected outcomes of moral behavior 36–7, 51, 75; toward potential regret 37–45, 49–51, 61, 74, 76, 78, *86*–*88*
aversion: loss- 11, 47; moral risk- 2, 5n17, 11, 32–53n41, 75–6, 101, 128–31, *86*, *88*; risk- 2, 5n17–18, 11, 14, 45, 47, 66, 101, 105, 107–10, 112, 115–6, 118

bargaining: fair nonarbitrary 70, 72, 77, 80, 82–4, 87, 102; power 80, 82–7; *see also* Principle of Fair Negotiation
beliefs, moral 12–4, 97, 102, 107, 115; *see also* attitudes
bias: confirmation 133; intergroup 14, 117; negativity 11, 47–8; status quo 47
The Bible 5n10, 30, 34, 133
Braintrust 116
Bruckner, D.W. 30–2

categorical: this book's theory as quasi- 65–8, 134; imperatives 66, 78, 111; morality as supposedly 129, 132–4; normativity 66, 133–4; rationality 26; *see also* attitudes
Categorical Imperative, Kant's 65, 100, 109, 134
Categorical-Instrumental Imperative: comparison to Kantianism 65–8; derivation of Four Principles of Fairness from 68–72; and moral psychology 87–*8*; and moral relevance 89n8, 103; overview of 61–65; revised defense of 72–6; unifying prudence, morality, and justice *86*, *88*
Christ, Jesus 26, 63
Churchland, P. 116–8
coercion 68–9, 71–2, 77, 80–84, *86*, *88*, 102, 118; *see also* Principle of Negative Fairness

cognition: moral 2–3, 8–15, 87–8, 100, 106–18; prudential 2–3, 8–15, 49–50, 86
cognitivism 14
commonsense 27, 42, 129
comparisons, interworld 28–9
compassion 63
compromise 70, 78–80, 105, 108–9
conditioning 2, 13–4, 103, 107, 116, 118
conflicts: and principles of fairness 69–70; social 79; value 103
conscience 41–3, 49–51, 88
consensus 65, 67, 70; see also agreement
consent 83
consequences: capacities for appreciating 9, 12, 104, 108; empirical regularities regarding 32, 36, 38, 42–3, 45–7, 50, 52, 73, 75, 77, 86; normative moral status of 118, 130; and psychopaths 9, 116; role in moral-prudential cognition 50, 88, 114–6, 130
consequentialism 106, 111, 115; see also utilitarianism
consolidation 13, 41, 44; see also learning, moral-prudential
constitutivism 14, 110–1, 133
constraints 2, 32, 51, 60, 66, 113, 129
contingencies, cross-temporal 13, 103, 110
contract 1, 31, 62, 82–8, 111–3; see also agreement; original position
contractarianism 1, 111–2, 114
contractualism 66, 106, 111–2, 114–5
cosmopolitanism 67, 84, 85–6, 88
costs 5n17, 11, 45, 69–71, 86, 101
counterexamples, potential 75–6, 128–31
cingulate gyrus (CG) 13, 103
criminality 9, 35, 40, 75
cross-cultural 34–6, 47
cuneus 13, 103

Dees, R. 74–77, 80–1, 83
Default Mode Network (DMN) 11–4, 101–4, 107, 110
decisions, big 28, 61
decision-theory 5n17, 74

deliberation 2, 31–2, 67–8, 71, 84, 105
demandingness 26, 89n8, 109, 113
desires: and the good 126; moral 36, 38–45, 48–51, 61–86, 88, 102; other-regarding 63–5, 86; prudent 36–9, 42–5, 46–8, 61, 72, 74, 77, 86; regarding the past and future 27, 61–4, 72–3, 74, 77–8, 86–89n8, 101–3, 106, 112; see also attitudes
development: moral-prudential 2, 32–45, 49, 52, 66, 71, 82, 103–4, 106–7, 130, 133; neurobehavioral 9, 104; see also learning, moral-prudential
dilemmas, moral 12
disagreement: moral 5, 69, 79, 82, 88, 114; philosophical 1, 3
discounting, temporal 10
dorsomedial prefrontal cortex (dmPFC) 12, 102

egocentricity 9; see also egoism
egoism 63–5, 70, 78–9, 86
emotion 10, 12–4, 31, 61, 63, 96, 104, 110, 114–6, 118, 130
empathy 10, 12–4, 78, 103–4, 114, 116–7
endorsement, reflective 110
endowment effect 47
ends 26–7, 65–8, 110, 127, 133
eudaimonia 1, 133
excellence 26, 108
explanation 2–3, 5, 95–7, 99–102, 105–6, 108–9, 111–2, 114–9
Explanatory Power 100, 105, 111, 113, 118
External Coherence 99, 105
extinction 12, 14, 102

fairness: to animals 71, 85, 90n26; intra and interpersonal 31, 64, 86; justice as 31, 83; principles of 26, 66, 68–72, 90n53, 113; prudential rationality of 73–80; in relationships 79, 83; Rightness as 66, 72, 74–77, 80–2, 84–6, 88, 89n8, 106, 108, 128, 134; social and political 80–7; to strangers

71; violations 29; virtues of 26; *see also* Four Principles of Fairness; *Prudence and Morality as Fairness to Oneself and Others*; Rightness as Fairness
fallacy, naturalistic 3, 126–7
family 33–4, 43, 67, 71, 81, 117
favoritism, temporal 28
fear 2, 11, 13–4, 33, 103–4, 107, 110, 112, 118
Firm Foundations 99–100, 105, 111, 113; *see also* Seven Principles of Theory-Selection
Four Principles of Fairness 2, 68–72, 74, 82, 84, *86*–89n8, 103: Principle of Fair Negotiation 70–1, 77, *86*–7, 89n8; Principle of Negative Fairness 69–71, 82; Principle of Positive Fairness 69–71, 82; Principle of Virtues of Fairness 70–1; *see also* Rightness as Fairness
freedom, transcendental 14, 110
Fruitfulness 7, 106, 113, 126; *see also* Seven Principles of Theory-Selection
fusiform gyrus (FG) 13, 102

gambling 13, 67, 77–8, 81, 103, 129; *see also* moral risk-aversion; risk-aversion
Gage, Phineas 13
good, the 28, 126
goodness, unconditional 110
Greene, J. 118
guilt 40–2, *44*, 38, *50*, 78, 102, 104

Hamlet 33–4
heaven and hell 36, *50*
hedonism 27
heroic fiction 34–5
Hitler, A. 76–7, 128
Holocaust, The 77, 131
Hubris Syndrome 104, 108, 130
Humean reduction 127

ideal theory 2, 85–*8*
imagination 9–10, 14, 67, 104, 107–8, 112, 118
immoralist 75, 77

immorality 33, 36–7, *39*, *41*, *44*–5, 47, *50*–1, 74–6, 78, 108, 129, 131
impulsivity 9, 38–*9*, 61
inferior temporal gyrus (ITG) 13, 102
infidelity 34, 42, *44*, 76–7
infinite 74, 97
inhibition, behavioral 11, 13, 104, 110
inner: monologue 12, 103, 107; satisfaction *39*, *41*, *44*, 48–*50*
instrumentalism: across human populations 26, 66, 104, 132; as dominant theory of normativity 26, 66; and moral cognition 45–*6*, 61–6, 68, 74–5, 77–80, 85, *86*, *88*, 104–6, 112–3, 117, 126–7, 130; and prudence 26–31, 45–*6*
insufficient reason, principle of 31
integrity 104
interests: altruistic 63–4, 69, 77–8; concerning costs 69, 79; desire to know one's future *50*, 61–3, 72–3, 78, *86*, *88*; estimating one's long-term 29; higher-order 68–9; egoistic 63–5, 70, 78; involuntary, semi-voluntary, and voluntary 61–5, 74; of one's possible selves 61–5, 67–70, 77, 112; other beings' 14, 67–8, 70, 77; other-regarding 63–5, 67, 70, 77; prudence as rational pursuit of 26–7; rationality of regarding as radically uncertain 30–1; shared 62; standing 27
Internal Coherence 99, 105
internalization 2, 32, 36–40, 43–*6*, 48–53n41, 60, 74–8, 84, *86*–*8*, 101–2, 104, 106–7, 116, 126, 128–9, 131, 133
interventions, experimental 9–10, 14, 102, 115
intuition 14, 115, 118
is-ought gap 3, 114, 126–7

judgment, moral 12, 97, 101, 114–6; *see also* attitudes; belief, moral
justice 1, 31, 36, 67, 69, 72, 82–*8*, 106, 132–3; *see also* fairness; Rightness as Fairness

Kant, I. 65, 67–8, 90n35, 109–10, 132, 134
Kantianism 26, 65–6, 100, 109–11, 132–4
Kelvans 130
kingdom of ends 65, 68

The Law of Peoples 85
learning, moral-prudential 2, 5n17, 9, 11–4, 26, 32–*46*, 48, 52, 53n41, 66, 76, 78, *86*–7 103–4, 106, 111, 116–7, 128–30, 133; *see also* development
LGBTQIA+ 81
likelihood 9, 29–37, 34, 36, 43–7, 49, 52, 62, 66, 71, 75, 87
lingual gyrus (LG) 13
lottery winners 29–30

martial arts 34
maximin 31
May, J. 115–6
mediocrity, moral 104, 108–9
memory 12–4, *39*, *50*–1, *88*, 102–4, 111, 115
meta-ethics 14
methods, philosophical 1–3, 129; *see also* Seven Principles of Theory Selection
#MeToo 76
middle occipital gyrus (MOG) 12, 102
middle temporal gyrus (MTG) 12, 102
Mill, J.S. 108
minimax: loss 31; regret 30–2, 35–6, *39*, 42, 45–*6*, 48–51, *86*
monologue, inner 12, 103, 107
Moore, G.E. 126
Moral Foundations Theory 115
morality: defined 1, 4; plays 32–7; as prudent life-strategy 30–*86*; unified with prudence and justice 82–7
morally-constrained utility maximization 45–*6*, *50*–1, *86*
Moral Original Position *see* original position
moral theories 4, 26, 106–14, 119, 126
motivation, moral 12–3, 61–6, 70, 72–*88*, 90n32, 96, 102, 107, 110–1, 114–6, 118, 125, 131–3
mutual advantage 79, 82, 102

negative fairness *see* Four Principles of Fairness
negotiation 70–2, 77–80, 82–3, *86*–9n8, 109, 118; *see also* agreement; bargaining; Four Principles of Fairness; Principle of Fair Negotiation
neural platform 116, 118
neuroessentialism 8
neurofunctional 2–3, 10–11, 60, 97, 101, 105–6, 113, 116, 118
nonideal theory 2, 85–*8*
normativity 4, 66, 110–1, 126–7, 129–30, 133–4
norms, moral 5n17, 9, 14, 32–5, 37–49, 61, 74, *86*, 104, 110–1, 116, 128–30

orbitofrontal cortex (OFC) 13, 103
original position: Cosmopolitan 84–*6*, *88*; Domestic 85–*6*, *88*; International 85–*6*, *88*; Moral 2, 67–71, 74, 82, *86*–*8*, 90n53, 101, 112, 133; Prudential 30–31, 36, 45–*6*, 82, 84, *86*, 111; Social-Political 2, 82, 84–5, 87, 106, 111; as unifying prudence, morality, and justice 83–*8*; *see also* Rightness as Fairness
other-perspective-taking (OPT) 9–10, 12, 14, 66, 101, 104–5, 107–8, 110, 112, 114–8, 130
outcomes: and cognition 9, 11, 13; expected, of moral behavior 32–49, 52, 74–5, 77–80, 128; nature of 27; prudence as maximizing expected 4, 26–32, 36, 45–*6*, *50*–51, 60, 66, 75, *86*–7, 108; radical uncertainty regarding 28–31
out-of-body experiences 12
oxytocin 116–8

pain 11, 27
Parsimony 100, 105, 109, 111, 113
performance, moral 9, 14, 104
phronesis 26
Plato 1, 132
planning 11, 14, 115

Index   143

pleasure 11, 27, 126
positive fairness *see* Four Principles of Fairness
poverty 82, 109
precuneus (PC) 13, 97, 102
predictions: of alternative theories 106–15; of this book's theory 45–52, *50*, *86–8*, 103–6, 130; counterfactual 2, 13
preference: reversals 30; satisfaction 27
Prichard, H.A. 132
Principle of Fair Negotiation 70–1, 77, *86–7*, 89n8
Principle of Negative Fairness 69–71, 82
Principle of Positive Fairness 69–71, 82
Principle of Virtues of Fairness 70–1
principles: of fairness 10, 26, 66 68–74, 77, 80, 82, 84–5, *86–9*n8, 90n53, 103, 105, 133; of justice 31, 67, *86–7*; moral 1, 10, 14, 45, 65–6, 68–72, 84, *86–8*, 104, 112, 114, 118, 131, 133; of prudence 31, 45–*6*, 68, 84, *86–8*; social-political 85–*8*; of theory selection 11–2, 68, 96–7, 99–100, 105, 111–3, 126, 129, 132, 134; *see also* Four Principles of Fairness; theory selection
privilege 79, 83
probabilities 29, 32, 67, 70–1
prospection 11, 14, 27, 30, *41*, *50*–1, 47, *88*, 103–4, 110
prudence: and behavioral neuroscience 4, 8–15, 101–6, 112, 115–8, 125–6; defined 1, 2, 26–8, 45; as distinct from morality 1, 126–7, 132–4; of moral risk-aversion 2, 5n17–18, 32–52, 128–31; and radical uncertainty 28–30, 45–*50*, 52, 63; and Rightness as Fairness 2, 61–5, 68–89n8; and social-political philosophy 2, 80–*8*; theory of 45–52; unified with morality 61–*88*, 101–6, 129–30, 133–4;

see also cognition; original position
Prudence and Morality as Fairness to Oneself and Others 95
psychology, moral and prudential *see* cognition
psychopathy 9, 11, 14, 38, 40, 48, 51, 66, 104, 110, 116, 118
punishment 13–4, 36–*41*, *44*, *50*–1, 78, 102, 104, 107, 112, 133

Quine-Duhem thesis 98

racism 79, *88*
rationalism 113–4, 116
rationality 26, 45–*6*, 49, 61, 68, 75–6, 80, *86*, 105–6, 108, 112–3, 128
Rawls, J. 31, 67, 82–5
realism, moral 113–4
reasonability 14, 112
reasoning 10, 45, 89n8, 95, 113–5, 118
reasons: epistemic 4, 68; moral 14, 113, 132–3; normative 1, 26, 112, 130, 133; prudential 3, 131
recognition: facial 12–3, 110; object 13; visual-word 13
redemption stories 35–8, 43, 47, *50*, 103
regret 9–11, 14, 30–9, 41–51, 60–2, 71–2, 74, 77–8, *86–9*n8, 101–4, 106, 110, 112, 116, 130–1; *see also* minimax regret
regularities, empirical 32, 36, 38, 42–3, 45–7, *50*, 52, 73, 75, 77, *86*
reinforcement 12, 38, 40, 103, 116, 134
relationships 42, *44*, 49, 52, 71, 83
relativity, theory of 98, 125
relevance: of empirical science 4; moral 62–5, 69–72, 89n8, 103
remorse 104
The Republic 132–3
reputation 43, 48
responsibility, moral 9, 117–8
retribution 79
retrospection 27, 30, *50*–1, *88*, 104
reward 10, 12–3, 36–*41*, *44*, 48, *50*, 102, 104, 133
rightness, moral 2, 72, 87

Rightness as Fairness: applying 82–*8*; critiques of 62, 68, 72, 74, 77, 80; overview of 61–72; revisions to 62–4, 70, 72, 77–87; and social-political philosophy 83–7; *see also* Categorical-Instrumental Imperative; Four Principles of Fairness; original position

Rightness as Fairness: A Moral and Political Theory 2, 60–2, 66, 68, 70, 72–4, 77, 89n8, 99, 130

risk-taking 11, 33–5, 102, 128–30; *see also* aversion

sacrifice 26, 35, 69, 78
sadness 13, 104, 110
self-awareness 12–4, 102
selfishness *see* egoism
self-preservation 11, 48, 80
selves: future 10, 12, 27–8, 51, 61–6, 69, 71–4, 77–81, *86*–9n8, 101–3, 105–6, 111, 115, 118, 134; morality as diachronic agreement between 62–72, 77–87, 101, 111, 118, 134; past 9–10, 13, 27–8, 31–2, 34, 36, *44*, 51, 63–4, 102, 103–4; problem of possible future 61–5, 72–6, 78, *86*–7, 89n8, 101–3, 106, 118
semantic 12, 127
sensitivity, moral 13–4, 103–4, 108, 110
sentimentalism 114–6
Seven Principles of Theory Selection 3–4, 99–100, 105, 112–3, 126, 129, 132, 134
sexism 79
sexual misconduct 43, 76
simulation, mental 8–10, 101, 104–5, 107, 109
Singer, P. 69, 109, 118
skepticism 1, 114, 132
slavery 77, 79, *88*
Smith, A. 5n18
Social Intuition Model 115
socialization 38, 104

social-political philosophy 2, 37, 72, 82–*8*, 106, 111
stages: of moral-prudential learning 38–*44*; person- 27, 31
Stoicism 1, 30–1, 132
stories 12, 14, 32–8, 43, 47, 97, 103; *see also* heroic fiction; redemption stories; tragedy
strangers 27, 51, 71
strict-compliance 67, 85–6
superior temporal sulcus (STC) 12, 102
sympathy 12, 14, 63

teleofunctional 4, 96
television 37–8, 130
test, moral 67, 74
temporal pole (TP) 12, 102
temporoparietal junction (TPJ) 10, 12, 14, 102, 107
A Theory of Justice 83, 85
theory of mind 12
theory selection *see* Seven Principles of Theory Selection
time-travel, mental 2, 8–10, 14, 66, 96, 101, 107–10, 115–8
tragedy 32–6, 43, *50*, 103, 129
transcranial magnetic stimulation 9–10, 14, 102, 115
transformative experiences 29–30

uncertainty: of life 28–30; and morality 61–64, 71, 73, 78, 81–2, 84, *86*–*8*, 102, 116, 129–31; and prudence 5n17, 30–2; 34–6, 45–*6*, 49–*50*, 52, 129–31
underdetermination 97–9
unification 66, *86*–*8*, 99–100, 105–6, 109, 111, 113, 115, 118
Unity 100, 105, 111, 113
universalizability 68, 100, 109
Utilitarianism 26, 31, 66, 108–9, 118; *see also* consequentialism
utility: aggregate lifetime 6n18, 27–30, 45–*46*, 51, 60, *86*; expected 45, 109; *see also* comparisons, interworld; utilitarianism

value: additive 28, 48; of ends 27; expected 11, 36, 45, 74–5; subjective 9, 13, 27, 29–30
veil of ignorance 31, 67–71, 82, *86*, *88*; see *also* original position
ventromedial prefrontal cortex (vmPFC): 12, 102
Viganò, E. 5–6n18

virtue ethics 66, 100, 106–8, 116; see *also* Aristotelianism
visual: memory 13, 104; processing 12–4

war 77, 79, 128, 131
well-being 1, 28, 29, 43, 48, 51, 75
Wernicke's area 12, 103
worry *see* anxiety

For Product Safety Concerns and Information please contact our EU representative GPSR@taylorandfrancis.com
Taylor & Francis Verlag GmbH, Kaufingerstraße 24, 80331 München, Germany

www.ingramcontent.com/pod-product-compliance
Lightning Source LLC
Chambersburg PA
CBHW051750230426
43670CB00012B/2221